Richard Hippisley Dominichetti

The Quest of Sir Bertrand

And Other Poems

Richard Hippisley Dominichetti

The Quest of Sir Bertrand
And Other Poems

ISBN/EAN: 9783744713436

Printed in Europe, USA, Canada, Australia, Japan

Cover: Foto ©Thomas Meinert / pixelio.de

More available books at **www.hansebooks.com**

THE QUEST OF SIR BERTRAND.

AND OTHER POEMS.

"SIR BERTRAND KNELT AT THE ABBEY GATE."

THE
Quest of Sir Bertrand,

AND OTHER POEMS.

BY

R. H. DOMENICHETTI.

WITH A FRONTISPIECE BY MRS. TRAQUAIR.

London:
W. H. ALLEN & CO., 13 WATERLOO PLACE.

AND AT CALCUTTA.

1890.

LONDON
PRINTED BY W. H. ALLEN AND CO., 13 WATERLOO PLACE,
PALL MALL. S.W.

CONTENTS.

CONTENTS.

LYRICS, &c.

ERRATA.

Page 79, line 7, *omit* by it

136. ,, 3, *for* aver *read* avow

THE QUEST OF SIR BERTRAND.

I.

Sir Bertrand knelt at the abbey gate ;
   In sorry plight was he :
He knocketh long, and yet may wait,
   Or ever it opened be.

Against the lintel of the door
   Weary he laid his face
All wan and white ; straight on before
   His wide eyes stared in space.

Soiled was his shining morion,
   And soiled his côte d'armure ;
The lions, wrought in gold thereon,
   Were dark with stains obscure.

THE QUEST OF SIR BERTRAND.

Dead thistles cumbered all the gate
    And withered hemlock tall,
With tangled nightshade lingering late
    Against the mouldering wall.

He knocketh until bolt and bar
    Long rusted gride and creak,
And standing by the door ajar,
    A cowléd monk 'gan speak.

"Now say, Sir Knight, wherefore dost stare
    With wide and awful eye?
There 's mire upon thine armour fair,
    Thy steed is fain to die."

"Assoil me, Father, if my sin
    May e'er assoiléd be,
And bless me, that I may begin
    My penance dread to dree."

" Nay, speak, my son ! no sin so dread,
  But may find boon of grace ;
God grant thy soul be comforted
  Or ere thou leave this place."

" O Father, Father ! though God's love
  Be wider than the sea,
And deeper than the waves thereof,
  There is no grace for me.

" On my black steed, nine years agone,
  Over the green hill-side
I rode from hunting all alone,
  At dewy eventide.

" I rode adown the wooded vale,
  In the solemn vesper hour ;
The twilight lingered faint and pale
  · By glade and trellised bower.

" I came unto a thicket close,
    Rich scent lay on the air,
  Cream-white and red the countless rose
    Bloomed forth, nor withered there.

" A wanton hymn slow-circled round,
    White limbs did softly gleam ;
  Like subtle scent, that airy sound
    Lulled me to drowsy dream.

" White arms were stretched to draw me in,
    Red lips they murmured ' Come ! '
  Ah ! Christ ! loud was the voice of sin,
    Thy face-veiled angels dumb !

" She led me to her lonely grot,
    She wove her mystic spell ;
  Full many a body there doth rot,
    Whose soul lies now in Hell."

" Now, Heaven shield thee, wretched wight,"
    Gasped forth the frightened priest.
" Nay, Father, ever day and night
    I lay, nor ever ceased

" The magic rune, that wove me round ;
    Her lips pressed close to mine,
In a dim web of sense and sound
    I lay for long years nine.

" Whether it was a voice from Heaven,
    Or pitying angel sent,
I know not, but the grace was given,
    And forth in shame I went."

Silence a moment lay on each ;
    Then faintly as in pain,
The monk one trembling hand did reach,
    But drew it back again.

" Arise ! my son, thy sin is deep,
    Yea, deeper than the sea ;
   But He, who heareth sinners weep,
     Will heal thy misery.

" Rise up, and in this holy place
    . Wrestle all night in prayer ;
   Perchance thou here may'st find the grace
     Shall make thee free as air."

Sir Bertrand rose, and in a dream
    Stooped through the lowly door :
With a dull lantern's wannish beam
    The pale monk went before.

So through the cloisters dark they came,
    Where moonbeams phantom-bright
Made spire and wall a wan white flame
    With shadows black as night.

And through the riven tracery
  He saw the shining sward,
And one shade deep as ebony,
  The spire that rose skyward.
    \

The church within was with incense dim,
  That round God's altar clings,
What time they echo to the hymn,
  God's shrines of evenings.

Through casements rich and far withdrawn,
  Moon-jewels faint and rare,
Like colours from a ghostly dawn,
  Glimmered adown the air,

Jacinth and topaz, amethyst
  And crimson deep as blood;
'Mid opal lights and pearly mist
  ˘ Uprose the Holy Rood,

With white Christ nailed in pain thereon;
   In that rich mystery,
It seemed a ray of Heaven was won
   To encircle Calvary.

And in the mystic gloom about
   The altar's silent throne
Glimmered seven lamps, nor e'er died out
   By day, nor midnight lone.

And spiring stone and carving rich,
   And fretwork frail as frost,
Rose up, with many a flowering niche,
   Like foam on darkness tost.

Silent they knelt in that dim place,
   When, lo! there faintly stole
A sound of singing heard in space;
   It tranced the listeners' soul.

'Twas **three** of God's own choristers
    Singing "Magnificat";
Blessed the voice that ministers
    God's House, and serves thereat!

For by the sweet high voice of praise
    This weary world is wrought
To harmony with angel lays,
    And Heaven on earth is brought!

"Gloria Patri!" sang the boys,
    Then ceased right suddenly:
A sound of shuffling feet, a noise
    Of chanting books laid by.

"Watch thou and pray," the pale monk said,
    "Endure the conflict keen;
The tempter whets his darts most dread
    'With thought of what has been.

" Resist his wanton lures and slay
    Thy lower self, that so,
  Where the dread tempest holds its sway,
    Thy soul unscathed may go.

" Spurn thou his wiles ; this wondrous woof,
    Woven of fleshly sense,
  Chains not his soul, who holds aloof
    From its dream-tissue tense.

" Watch thou and pray ! and here subdue
    Thyself, and die to live
  A holier life 'mid lights anew,
    Than realms of sense can give."

  Alone in that vast place he lay,
    With parchéd lips and sere ;
  His desert soul knew not to pray,
    Athirst for one cool tear.

Then wicked memories hot like flame
    Thrilled through him, wild and sad
His youth's dead passions whirling came
    In wanton dances mad.

" Thine, are we thine ! and thou art ours ;
    That ruined soul resign,
Where erst through dim voluptuous hours
    We reigned for long years nine ! "

Pale-eyed he fought them off as one,
    Bent to some toil he plies
At harvest time beneath the sun,
    Beats off the swarm of flies.

Slow stole the dawn and steeped in light
    Each clustered shaft and aisle,
And from their lofty vantage height
    The stern-faced seraphs smile.

Sir Bertrand gazed with tearful eyes
  Where at the altar stood
A priest, clad all for sacrifice
  Of Christ's Body and Blood.

The Mass was said, he bowed his head,
  God's blessing to receive ;
Within his soul a still voice said,
  " My son ! no longer grieve ! "

II.

Unto the western porch he came,
  Where stood the monk in prayer,
Nor marked how with a clear pale flame
  The sunlight warmed the air.

Ever upon his breviary
  His steadfast eyes were bent,
Where colours like an evening sky
  With holy words were blent.

"Benedicite ! " the pale monk said,
   "Yon path by the hawthorn hedge
Leads to the deep green valley's head,
   And on by the steep slope's edge.

"In the valley green the Hermit dwells
   In his cave by the streamlet's rim,
Faintly he hears our abbey bells
   By morn and twilight dim.

"Give greeting unto the holy sage,
   Unfold thy woeful tale ;
He only may read thy life's dark page,
   The Hermit of the vale."

The warrior turned with one farewell,
   And held his charger's rein :
In haste he wended the wide green fell,
   Nor once looked back again.

Now journeying by a pathway dim
   Adown the wooded hill,
He marked, amid the tree-trunks slim,
   The sparkle of a rill.

It was a fair deep-bosomed vale,
   Where dewy-dim did dream
The April woods, all green and frail,
   Beside the winding stream.

O'er rounded stones the waters fall,
   The primrose pale doth star
Each shadowed slope, the cuckoo's call
   Rings vaguely from afar.

Or 'mid the hawthorn clusters white
   Fluteth the throstle soft,
And swallows in swift steel-blue flight
   Circle and swoop aloft.

Both knight and war-horse pacing slow
  Felt a soft influence thrill
Through every limb with subtle glow,
  The fire of gay April.

He thridded the silver beechen boles,
  Mantled with green bright moss :
Shy conies peered from sandy holes,
  Or darted his path across.

The squirrel leapt from bough to bough
  Of the dark and stately fir ;
So still was the air, thou mightst avow
  The grass did scarcely stir.

The underwood lay a frail green haze,
  Beyond blue hills were seen,
Adown the leaf-strewn forest ways,
  Through the budding alder screen.

" Yon grassy bend of the rivulet
        Should be the Hermit's home ;
    The tired soul here might well forget
        All else, nor seek to roam ! "

    Sheer rose o'erhead the scarpéd rock
        Shrouded with branch and brier,
    Rent by an ancient tempest shock,
        Or bolt of thunder-fire.

    The cavern's mouth was screened from sight
        With ivy and eglantine ;
    'Mid moss and fern the lichens bright
        Like gold and topaz shine.

    Snowdrop and yellow aconite,
        Crocus and daffodil,
    Lay round like flakes of starry light
        Reflected in the rill.

Within his cell the Hermit sat,
   A Book upon his knee;
Ever his deep eyes pored thereat,
   For love of Grammarye.

The tome was old and claspéd fair
   With clasps of graven brass;
A butterfly most debonnair
Had fluttered down and quivered there,
   While a minute's space might pass.

His beard, more white than winter snow,
   Rested upon the page;
Keen were his eyes and bright, I trow
   He was a winsome sage.

All on his table rude there lay
   A skull with fleshless eyes,
And garlands fresh of flowerets gay,
   A cross and rosaries.

Green moss grew o'er the rugged floor,
　　Green ferns waved from the wall ;
No richer mantlet covers o'er
　　Bower or monarch's hall.

"Now, hail to thee, thou holy man ! "
　　" Sir Knight, peace be with thee ! "
Thus with calm words the sage began,
　　As he looked up steadfastly.

His eyes shone bright beneath his brow :
　　" What quest is thine, Sir Knight ?
Thine armour and tabaret avow
　　Thou 'rt come from grievous fight."

" Nay, Father, it is no body's pain,
　　Or tourney wound I bring ;
But a sick soul that sighs in vain
　　For shrift and houseling."

Then with choked voice and bitter tears
   He told his woful tale:
The Hermit soothes his anguished fears,
With words of holy lore he cheers
   The stricken warrior pale.

" Great is thy sin ; but out of sin
   By wondrous alchemy
God doth his brightest jewels win,
   To set them in the sky.

" Five senses fine to man were given
   For service and delight,
Channels, whereby God's earth and heaven
   Might flood his soul with light.

" That sweetest sound and light serene
   And scents and colour rare,
Like a wavering veil might hang between,
Nor hide, but shadow forth th' unseen
   With imagery fair.

2 *

" **But sin,** like a noisome taint, did **stain**
  Man's nature's holiest springs
With **its** heritage of mystic pain
  And dark foreshadowings.

" **And** loveliness to him became
  A garish false delight,
Alluring like the restless flame
  That mocks the marsh **by** night.

" Nathless to him who, spite of **fears,**
  Hath turned his heart to God,
There 's pleasure in frail gossamers
  That glisten on the sod ;

" There 's healing in the fresh **green leaves,**
  Blithe music in the brook ;
Through pathways five his soul receives
  The vision it forsook.

" Such blithesome joy of **innocence**
    Not thine it is to gain,
  Only by bitter penitence
    To purge that one foul stain.

" Yet may'st thou still, at intervals
    Of thy dark spirit's strife,
  Listen unto the strain that falls
    Like dew on thy bare life.

" Still may'st **thou** list the jargoning,
    The sweet birds make in May :
  'Mid fires of God's own sunsetting
    Thou may'st kneel down and pray.

"**And yet** thy wounded heart may beat
    For all who travail sore,
  The weary, weary, world-worn feet,
    The wide world lies before."

In louring gloom the twilight sank,
    The night waxed drear and dim,
A chill breeze swayed the grasses rank
    Beside the streamlet's rim.

"Now, list, sir Knight," the Hermit said,
    " To-night shalt thou keep tryst
'Neath the hawthorn tree, in holy dread,
    Hell's power to resist.

" At dawn, if thou hold leal and true,
    Christ's pardon will I bring,
And rede thee the penance thou must do
    For thy soul's houseling."

The moon's white face with rain was wet,
    Half-veiled in cloud and mist,
She glanced amid the branchéd net,
    And the gnarléd hawthorn kist.

Sir Bertrand knelt with eyes upturned,
  Bathed in the broken gleams,
Like crystal through his tears they burned,
  Beneath the moon's pale beams.

Then on a sudden was he 'ware
  How 'neath that ancient tree,
With white arms stretched and shadowy hair,
  There stood a fair ladye.

Her full throat thrilled, as though she sobbed,
  E'en softlier than the dove,
And, passion-wrung, her bosom throbbed
  With tender plaint of love.

" Alack ! Sir Knight, thou faithless heart,
  Why didst thou leave me lorn ?
Ah ! woe is me for the bitter smart,
  That hath my heart-strings torn ! "

E'en as she spoke she nearer drew,
　　And her bosom, white and warm,
Beamed through the shadow on his view,
　　As she raised her rounded arm.

"Heaven is a hollow phantasy
　　Save on these lips and breast ;
Hell's fire is where pale lovers sigh,
　　Whose pains can find no rest.

"Weary the pilgrimage thereof,
　　Yet here his inmost shrine,
Where burn the deathless fires of Love
　　Within this heart of mine !

"What, wouldst thou spurn the rose full blown,
　　Because its heart is red,
Or press the thorns into thine own,
　　Or crown therewith thine head ?"

His eyes were wild, his cheek grew wan,
   The sweat-drops large and bright
Stood out his anguished brow upon,
   Death-pale in the pale moonlight.

"Temptress! Avaunt! That honeyed smile
   Masks death and hell.   Avaunt!
Seek not to lure with wanton wile
   The soul thou didst enchaunt."

Swift as the storm, an awesome light
   Glared in the lady's face,
And marred her bloom, like a deathful blight
   Shrouding her beauty's grace.

"A malison! a malison!
   "For the craven Knight," she cried;
Then chill stood she as carven stone,
   On her lips the wild curse died.

With faltering hand the Knight did sign
　　His brow with the Holy Rood ;
By might of that amulet divine
　　The witch affrighted stood.

Wan grew her brow, and wan her eyes ;
　　With a piercing shriek, I wist,
She faded away, as at sunrise
　　Fadeth the white marsh-mist.

Forspent and worn, with brain o'erwrought,
　　Like a sculptured statue lay
The Knight, bereft of sense and thought,
　　Until the break of day.

'Mid drizzly mist the hawthorn stood,
　　With budding leaflets green ;
Gnarléd and black its antique wood
　　Glistened with raindrops' sheen.

Anon the sun rose merrily,
  The branches' frail green fret
Glittered like blithesome jewelry
  With emeralds overset.

The Hermit riseth with the lark
  That from wet grasses springs,
And a challenge to the flying dark
  In joyance wildly flings.

'Neath the hawthorn tree the Hermit spied
  Where the Knight lay on the grass :
" Alack, alack ! " aloud he cried,
  " Woe 's me for this sad pass ! "

He set the Knight's head on his knee,
  The face showed white like death,
Yet 'twixt the pale lips fitfully
  Laboured the hard-drawn breath.

He drew from his vest a clear phial
  Of crystal fair and bright,
And set to his lips a cordial
  Of strange and wondrous might.

Each drop shone in the pale sunshine
  Like amber, as it fell,
Distilled from herbs of Palestine
  By Paynim infidel.

Slow stole the blood into his cheek,
  That death-pale was afore,
But faint and weak, a fitful streak,
  A far wave on life's shore.

The Hermit loosed his gorget close,
  And eke his côte d'armure;
With white lips doth the Knight disclose
  His grisly aventure.

"Courage, my son! The fight is won,
    By shrift is thy spirit cleared;
Last night I heard, in deep vision,
    The angels chant thy weird.

"Seven years shalt thou wander to and fro,
    With worn and weary feet,
Until this hawthorn-staff shall blow,
Whereby thy ransomed soul may know
    Thy penance is complete."

"A saying hard is this, I ween!
    Yet a stranger miracle,
Than for yon staff to bud in green,
    My soul hath known right well!"

"The word that bade my barren soul
    Burst forth from sin's dread power,
May bid this withered sap unfold
    Leaflet and silver flower."

"Well said, my son; now haste thee don
    These weeds of Palmer gray,
  And eke these Pilgrim shoon bind on:
    God speed thee on thy way!

"Thy goodly steed that here doth feed
    With thee this day must go:
  Of him the Master hath some need,
    Which thou eftsoons shalt know.

"Farewell! farewell! God guard thee well!"
    With tears the Hermit cried.
"Farewell, farewell to thy blithesome dell,
    Blessings to thee betide.

"Oh! gay mine armour burnished bright,
    And gay my coat of gold;
  But never beat my heart so light
    As 'neath this russet fold."

III.

The morning skies lay far outspread,
  Cloud above pearly cloud ;
Faint rainy lights yet lingeréd
  Amid their fleecy shroud.

Sir Bertrand gazed, and unto him
  It seemed a city fair
Rose faint and far, with gateways dim
  And bulwarks built of air.

Wide alleys there the sun's pale gold
  Glinted full softly down ;
And a stream of palest azure rolled
  Midmost that faery town.

Dim were his eyes with vague desires,
  While through the dawnlight chill
Rang, like a thousand golden lyres,
  The birds' song clear and shrill.

And now his path lay straight and clear
  Upon the high road white :
The Palmer turned, a bitter tear
  Bedimmed his yearning sight.

" Farewell, farewell, thou blithesome dell,
  Before the wide world lies !
Still haunt of peace, farewell, farewell ! "
The parting words rang like a knell,
  That tolls when a sweet soul dies.

The dull thud of his charger's feet
  Smote on the high-road dry ;
It seemed each beat did still repeat
  That farewell changelessly.

As thus he wended sad and slow,
  Holding his charger's rein,
A voice from the wayside hailed him low,
  The moan of one in pain.

" Sir Palmer, a boon, for love of Heaven!
    Sir Palmer, of thy good grace
  Have pity, as thou wilt be forgiven
    Before God's holy face."

"Now say what boon thou poor lepér
    Thou cravest of charity ;
  No alms have I, these weeds aver
    I can no poorer be ! "

" No alms crave I, thou Palmer Gray,
    But a ride on thy good steed ;
  My feet faint sore on the King's highway,
    As well thine eye may rede."

" Now haste thee up, thou poor lepér,
    Now haste thee up and ride ;
  I had liefer far thou shouldst sit there
    Than a king in all his pride."

The Lazar's limbs ran foul with sores,
    Withered and leprous-white ;
The noisome plague in his body's pores
    Lay like a festering blight.

The face it was a ghastly thing ;
    In its features worn and lean
The seal of God's own hand-making
    Might hardly there be seen.

Deep groaned he as in deadly pain,
    His weary head was bent,
Yet his parched lips breathed forth no plain
    For God's scourge on him sent.

As thus their toilsome way they made,
    A merry rout flashed by,
A gallant knight and cavalcade
    Of flaunting chivalry.

Full loud they laughed, in scornful way,
    " A goodly pair ! " they cried,
" The leper man and the Palmer Gray,
    And the leper man doth ride ! "

Swift flashed they by with noise and glare,
    And nought doth there remain
But clouds of dust upon the air
    That dwindle down the plain.

" So passeth this world's pomp and pride,"
    Quoth the Palmer 'neath his breath ;
" Like dust the wind doth puff aside,
    The viewless wind of death ! "

Now journeying they might descry
    The high walls of a town,
With four tall spires against the sky
    And slant roofs lower down.

St. Mary's spire, St. Martin's spire,
    St. James's steeple high,
And the gilded vane that shines like fire
    Upon the tall belfry.

"Oh! yonder lies the goodly town,
    Its belfries one may count!"
"Good Palmer, I prithee set me down,
    Here would I fain dismount."

One hand he laid on saddle-bow,
    And his arms about him cast;
The leper breatheth weak and low,
    As each breath were his last.

Sudden there beamed a heavenly light,
    The leper was no more,
His raiment shone as angel's bright,
    That tattered was afore.

His face all lovely, washed of tears,
   That no cloud now doth mar,
Unworn by all the pilgrim years,
   Shone brighter than a star.

That face, fulfilled with heavenly light,
   Absorbed in its bright beams
The Palmer's face, upturned and white,
   Rapt, as in wondrous dreams.

Dread, beautiful and sadly sweet
   The moments mystical,
When drowséd day and twilight meet,
   Sun-flushed at evenfall.

But lovelier yet and sweeter still
   Than twilight's soft embrace,
The rapture that his soul did fill,
   In the light of God's own Face.

From piercéd Hands and Feet and Side
    Five rosy rays did smite,
Seal of the God-love crucified,
    A carcanet of light.

The gracious Guest hath gently prest
    With words of mercy fain
That drooping head unto His Breast,
    Where it hath gladly lain.

" My rule is o'er the poor and sad,
    My realm the silent bourn,
Where patient sorrow maketh glad,
    The land of those who mourn."

One instant ere his brain did swoon,
    O'erwrought with ecstasy,
Through prison-bars of flesh a tune
    He heard fall from the sky.

'Twas angels seven, who sang in heaven
   Their glorious roundelay,
Rejoicing o'er one soul forgiven,
   Whose sins are washed away.

To earth he sank, those dear Hands move
   In blessings o'er his head ;
There in an ecstasy of love
   Long lay he, as one dead.

When that his wondering eye did ope,
   A chapel fair he spied,
Hard by the road on grassy slope;
   Thither straightway he hied.

As he knelt before the stone chapell
   In joy and wonderment,
Rang shrill and clear a silver bell ;
Ever it ringeth that men may tell
   Passeth God's Sacrament.

Twain and twain the fair boys came,
   White-stoled and torch in hand ;
Redly blew back the scented flame,
   By breeze of morning fanned.

Under a silken canopy
   The Priest did slowly tread :
The Sacred Host he bare on high
   Unto some dying bed.

The Palmer Gray, he smote his breast,
   Bent low for reverence,
He felt the stir of silken vest,
   The fume of sweet incense.

" Sir Priest ! a boon, a boon ! " he cried,
   " For His sake thou dost bear.
  Mount up, Sir Priest, mount up and ride
    Upon my charger fair ! "

"A blessing on thee, Palmer Gray,
    For thy holy charity ;
I wend afar a lonesome way,
    Where a sick soul doth sigh.

The boys have ta'en the goodly steed
    And set the Priest thereon ;
The Palmer now in very deed
Hath holpen his dear Lord in need,
    And on his way hath gone.

The Palmer crossed the drawbridge strong,
    And wendeth on apace;
No heed he payeth the giddy throng,
    His cowl drawn o'er his face.

Minstrels and jesters, troubadours,
    Jongleurs in gaudy dress,
Men of light songs and light amours,
    Leapt up and down the press.

With twang of wire sweet rhymes they sung
　Unto the fair ladies,
Who roses to the minstrels flung
　O'er arrassed balconies.

From street to street 'twas pleasaunce all,
　Like wayward rivulet,
The townsfolk pass without the wall,
　The tourney-lists are set.

Two and two the Knights do ride,
　With jingling spur and chain ;
Their chargers champ with haughty pride,
Two pages pace on either side,
　Holding the bridle-rein.

And pennons fair flap in the air,
　Wrought with strange imagery
Of beast and bird ; the burghers stare
　To see the knights pass by.

Amid the rout the Palmer stood
   Astonied with the din;
His face was covered with his hood,
   You scarce might see his chin.

A jester with his staff and bell
   Smote him and idly jeered:
" Thou hidest that face of thine right well,
   Yet one may see thy beard! "

With cheer and shout the burghers cried,
   " Away, thou Palmer Gray! "
They bore him off upon the tide
   Unto the tourney gay.

The lists were set in meadows green,
   A river circled round;
Full many a good knight there, I ween,
   Would bite the meadow ground!

The seats were hung with arras rich,
  The damsels chattered bold ;
Deep in her dim embroidered niche
  The Queen sat all in gold.

The chargers pawed the dust and neighed,
  Rich housings swept the ground ;
Loudly each brazen trumpet brayed,
In rest each glittering lance was laid,
  In answer to the sound.

Then closed the lines like thunder-cloud,
  'Mid blare of trumpet-blast ;
Like foam the white plumes swayed and bowed,
  And glittering spears were brast.

These sights and colours that they prize
  Seem unto him, as one
Who from the sun's glare shuts his eyes,
And sees its spangled phantasies
  About him reel and run.

The Palmer thridded the gaping throng
   And hied to a convent fair ;
There in the dark church all night long
   He knelt in silent prayer.

IV.

The Palmer Gray hath journeyed far,
   All unto fair Cologne,
Where those three pilgrims of the star
   In stately shrine are shown.

Full piously his tears did fall,
   And gazed he long on them ;
" A weary pilgrimage withal
   Ye made to Bethlehem ! "

The Palmer Gray hath journeyed south
   To Saint James of Compostelle,
Whose glory speeds from mouth to mouth
   With dower of miracle.

And where in jewelled fretwork rich,
    Amid the tapers' shine,
St. Mark doth rest in sainted niche,
    His pious knees incline.

And now unto the Holy Land,
    That blessed ground to greet,
By day and night, o'er trackless sand,
    Travail his wayworn feet.

Bare glisters now the desert wide,
    White glares the sun at noon ;
" Alack ! " the woful pilgrim cried,
    " Death will come all too soon ! "

Yet oft by night the silver beams
    Of the moon enwoven were,
A ladder frail, that angel-dreams
Glimmered adown 'mid pearly gleams,
    God's love to minister.

Seldom with sound like silver bell,
  The babbling waters rise,
With palms slow-heaving on the swell,
  Beneath the hard blue skies.

Yon little cloud, what may it mean,
  On the far desert's rim ?
It speedeth fast, and now, I ween,
The sun beat sharp on lances keen
  'Mid whirling dust-wreaths dim.

And now the Palmer seeth plain
  The Paynim chivalry
Bear down on him with loosened rein,
  Like a bolt from out the sky.

Both hand and foot they bound him fast
  Unto their saddle-bow.
At eve the wretched wight they cast
  In prison dark and low.

Therein for many weary years
  A Red Cross Knight had lain,
Rising at night with bitter tears,
And crying out, where no man hears,
  In piteous longing vain.

Within the dungeon dark and deep
  Full many a year they lay,
Beneath the Paynim's strongest keep,
  Far from the lightsome day.

Nathless the dawn through stanchion high
  Shone blue as any gem,
And when the cool dark night drew nigh,
  One star looked down on them.

No face they saw, no sound they heard,
  Save from the garden fine,
Unseen there sang some wondrous bird,
  That dwells in Palestine.

Also what time the palace rang
   With dance and merriment,
They heard the brazen cymbals clang,
   Where'er the Paynim went.

Faintly at sunset cinnamon
   And balsams rich and rare,
Made sickly by the summer sun,
   Stole to them on the air.

At dawn and eve they chanted sweet
   Roundels of days bygone,
And oft-times would their lips repeat
   Our Lady's Antiphon.

The Paynim's daughter paced at morn
   Along the garden-close,
And, turning to her maids high-born,
   Asked them, "What strains be those?"

Then spake straightway her fair ladies,
   "Two Christian knights, pardie,
Chaunt ballads sad and love ditties
    To loves they ne'er shall see."

At eve the Princess with her train,
   'Mid scent of musk and myrrh,
Walked with her maidens three, the strain
   Rose sad and sweet to her.

" Nay, by my troth, these Christian men,
   Unto their loves be true,
I trow the fickle Saracen
   Had found him heartsease new ! "

" Unto the dungeon will I go,
   And see this sweet minstrel ;
My golden state I 'ld leave, to know
   His secret strong love-spell."

When that the morrow's sun did dawn,
  The weary prisoners twain
Heard rusted bolt and bar withdrawn,
  Down dropt the heavy chain.

The blessed light full strong and bright
  Smote down upon their eyes,
So that all dazzled was their sight,
  Nor aught could they surmise.

Midmost there stood upon the stairs,
  Where the dark gates unclose,
With pitying face a lady fair,
  Holding a fresh-plucked rose.

Her maidens twain, on either hand,
  Were well-nigh fair as she,
Be sure, they deemed that there did stand
  A heavenly company.

" Alack ! " cried one, " 'tis Mary Queen
    With her twain handmaidens,
Catherine and Cecily." I ween
    Astonied was his sense.

The vision spake ; her sweetest voice
    Was like the merry tune
Wherewith the blithesome birds rejoice
    The thickets close on June.

Softly she questionéd wherefore
    They sang so sweet and clear,
That whoso passed their grille before,
    Halted the strain to hear.

" What love," quoth she, " hath power to live
    In this so gloomy cell ?
Much gold and silver would I give
    To rede thy wondrous spell."

Then did the Palmer tell of Her
    Whom all true Christians love,
Round whom the bright choirs minister,
    The Queen of Saints above :

Sweet mother-maid, whose tresses gold
    Fall o'er her broidered vest,
While wrapt within her bosom's fold
    Her Babe is lulled to rest.

In wonder then the Princess cried
    " I would some image see,
Whereby in truth might be descried
    Thy sick brain's phantasy ! "

The Princess parted therewithal
    With her handmaidens twain,
And lock and bar with clangour fall,
    And all is dark again.

Within the cell a pillow rude
  Of shapeless wood there lay,
Oft by the Palmer's tears bedewed
  At eve and break of day.

From this he strove with labour vain
  To fashion forth his thought;
Toil as he might, yet all his pain
  No glad fruition brought.

Weary he wrought till close of day,
  Then laid his tools aside,
With aching heart to kneel and pray,
  At fall of eventide.

The twilight stole, all hushed and dim,
  O'er the rose-garden fair ;
The Palmer chanteth his vesper hymn,
  And kneeleth down in prayer.

" Mary Queen, the night draws nigh
    To those in bondage stress ;
Bend thy sweet face from the sky,
    And our travail bless ! "

At deep midnight our Lady came,
    Bright seraphs round her played,
With wings that now in crimson flame,
    Now into twilight fade.

The beauteous vision stretched her hand
    And touched the shapeless wood ;
Lo ! straight in her fair likeness planned
    A heavenly image stood.

The jewelled pinions round her whirl,
    The fiery colours blink,
Like hues of sunset softly furl,
    And into darkness sink.

Pale glanced the dawn through prison-bars,
   The Palmer oped his eye,
And marked the last faint steely stars
   Yet lingering in the sky.

All in the pallid light he sees
   A beauteous image gleam,
Where late he wrought upon his knees,
And wrought with empty toil to seize
   An ever-fleeting dream.

The Princess came at fall of eve
   Unto the dismal cell ;
Scarce could her wondering eyes believe
   The gracious miracle.

With reverence and holy fear
   The Palmer told his dream,
And as he spake, a crystal tear
   Adown her cheek did stream.

He told her then of Bethlehem,
   And eke of Calvary:
Be sure, the angels gazed on them,
   Rejoicing in the sky.

Thereat her faith waxed firm and strong,
   She loathed her palace bowers;
For Christian ways her soul did long,
   Through all the weary hours.

Unto the prisoners twain she cried,
" Arise, at midnight deep
Three steeds by the postern gate abide,
   The guards shall soundly sleep! "

At deep midnight the prisoners twain
   Heard rusted bolt and bar
Fall down, and there unveiled again
   They gazed on sky and star.

Like shadows by the wall they glide
    Unto the postern gate ;
By the castle wall three steeds abide,
    The Princess there doth wait.

The holy image still she bare,
    Close to her bosom prest,
Rich jewels glittered in her hair,
    And sparkled from her vest.

" To our Lady Queen, the Ransomer,
    A dowry rich I bring ;
Not empty-handed I come to her,
    The daughter of a king."

The moon glanced through a cloudy rift,
    And the castle-bell did sound ;
The Lady to her steed they lift,
    Their horses spurn the ground.

Swift, swift they fly o'er the desert wide
Blanched by the pale moonlight.
On! on! their phantom shadows glide,
The sand flies in their flight.

" Away! away! ere break of day
We reach the Pilgrims' well!"
And ever on deserts blank the ray
Of level moonlight fell.

Pale-green the dawn awakening
Glimmered along the sky,
Like depths of ocean wavering
In mellow mystery.

Fierce glared the sun at noonday high,
The trackless desert shone,
The reddening sun sank down the sky,
And day was well nigh done.

When lo! against a liquid band
    Of primrose colour clear,
Tall palms by eve's slow breezes fanned,
    At close of day draw near.

A crystal well, a mossy bank,
    And green delicious shade ;
The weary fugitives down sank
    In the soft-shadowed glade.

Outwearied was each gallant steed,
    Panting and fain to fall ;
Pursuers nigh, in bitter need
    To heaven for help they call.

Fearful they laid them down to sleep,
    Midmost the desert vast ;
The slow wind wending night's great deep
    Sighed gently as it past.

When dawn with bird's song softly rose,
  The pilgrims, fearful yet,
From slumber now their eyes unclose;
  What sight their wonder met ?

All on a fair green knoll they lay,
  With daisies pied and starred ;
Over the valley peered the day,
  Through cloudlets white and barred.

With blithesome note the rivulet
  Rippled through birchen shade ;
Around the leaf-hid violet
  Scented the budding glade.

The Red Cross Knight in wild amaze
  Leapt up, and loud he cried :
" Wander we yet in sleep's dim maze
  Upon the desert wide ?

" Oh ! yonder lies my castle strong,
 And there the village mill
Tells to the dawn its undersong
  Beside the lilied rill ! "

There stood those three, nor moved one limb,
 For fear the dream should fail ;
As one who in sleep's valley dim
Clasps some dead lover unto him
 With love's wild hunger pale.

On emerald slope, girt round with yew,
 Uprose the grey church spire ;
About the tower the jackdaws flew,
 The windows shone like fire.

" Glory to God and our Ladye ! "
 With joy the Pilgrims cried,
And swift unto the grey belfry
 Adown the vale they hied.

Without the sun lay broad and strong
   Upon the graveyard green ;
The bells their solemn peal prolong
   Amid the yew tree's screen.

Within the light was dim and faint,
   The tapers twinkle bright ;
With golden cloths embroidered quaint
   The altar was bedight.

Sudden upon the morning still,
   A chant rose fitfully ;
Adown the valley, o'er the hill,
   The lingering echoes die.

Through hawthorn branches budded white,
   Black robes and white were seen,
And a golden cross that glimmered bright,
   Atween the clustered green.

Along the daisied slope they wend
  Through spring's soft light and shade,
Beside the rippling streamlet's bend,
While dim blue incense wreaths ascend
  And into thin air fade.

First three fair boys the censer swung,
  And then devout and pale
The pure-faced nuns their anthems sung,
  Beneath their wimpled veil.

Next six handmaids in lily white
  The path with flowers did strew,
Lilies and roses, vermeil-bright,
  New washed in morning dew.

And in their midst, clad like a bride,
  A lady still and fair,
Like some white spirit on did glide,
  With many a murmured prayer.

And now they reach the portal dark,
   And enter one by one ;
The dim aisle gleams with taper's spark,
   The nuns their chant intone.

The Priest hath at the altar bowed
   God's rite to minister ;
The white-robed choristers sing loud,
   And swing the gold censér.

With lips and cheeks like ivory,
   And eyes far off and large,
The lady knelt, like those who see
   Loom nigh death's lone sea-marge.

Low laid like corpse for burial rite
   The lady then they shroud ;
At feet and head a burning light,
The death-pall is with flowerets dight,
   Rose-lights on wannest cloud.

And ever as they placed and flung
   Bright blossoms on the bier,
A tender ditty thus they sung
   In accents soft and clear :—

" *Lilies white and virginal*
   Strew we thus upon thy pall ;
Roses red like drops of blood
   Fallen from the holy rood ;
And white roses pale and faint,
   Like some fair ecstatic saint ;
Heartsease purple for a token
   Of the balm for sad hearts broken ;
And, for pain to pilgrim due,
   Rosemary and bitter rue.
Bride of Christ, these earthly flowers
   Wither in wet autumn hours ;
But the blooms of paradise
   Soon shall gladden weary eyes ;
There bright beds of marigold
   Our dear Lady's throne enfold,

And her lilies marble-white
Lift their coronals of light,
Strewn with gold-dust from the heart,
Where the silver petals part."

The Red Cross Knight, as in a trance,
  Beholds the white robes wave ;
Before his eyes the tapers dance,
  The chants like billows rave.

Nought clear but that white form he sees,
  The fair lost face that still,
Like the mirrored moon on dreary seas,
  His bondage dreams did fill.

Sudden he strides to the altar stair,
  With voice like trumpet tone
He quells the sweet response and prayer ;
  The warrior stood alone.

5 *

Deep silence fell on all that throng,
    So that each one tongue-tied
Might hear the twittering chirping song
    The small birds made outside.

He rent the cerecloth from her face,
    And cried, " My love, awake ! "
" My wife ! my love ! " the blood apace
    On her cheek like dawnlight brake.

Surely she deemed his spirit blest
    Beckoned from Paradise ;
Till closely to his bosom prest,
    Her face in rapture lies.

What need to tell how thence did fare
    The knight and his ladye
Unto their home, with trumpet blare
    And merry minstrelsy ?

The Red Cross Knight with loving guile
   Oft-times the Palmer prest,
" Bide with us here a little while,
   Bide with us here and rest."

But aye the Palmer said him nay,
   With tears upon his cheek :
" No rest for me upon my way
   Save in the heaven I seek."

The Paynim princess bideth there
   With our Lady of Liesse ;
She hath shorn away her raven hair,
And vowed a life of holy prayer,
   Her heart's love to express.

By hawthorn glade in summer green
   Uprose a convent fair ;
The grey walls there may yet be seen,
   A house of chaunt and prayer.

The convent bells sound sweet and deep,
    The poor those grey walls bless,
Solace of all sad eyes that weep,
    Our Lady of Liesse!

On the low hill the Pilgrim stood,
    A figure lone and dim,
And on his left, as red as blood,
    Sank down the broad sun's rim.

The twilight lay, dim-fretted gold,
    All o'er the vague dark plain,
Where now the sheep unto their fold
    Were wending back again.

Swift falls the night, the sunset fades
    Into the last gold ray;
The Pilgrim, 'mid eve's closing shades,
    Pursues his darkening way.

V.

Now unto Rome the Pilgrim wends,
   Wherein St. Peter reigns ;
Thither his way-worn steps he bends,
And blithely now his hymn ascends
   Upon the lonesome plains.

Wide green waste places, whereon lie
   Temple and ruined shrine :
Wide wastes of sultry purple sky,
   And wide waste pools that shine.

The white mist gathers o'er the waste,
   Blotting its vivid green
And polished pools.   On, Pilgrim, haste !
   Or night will intervene !

But now at sultry fall of even
   He sees the city loom
Against a fiery rift of heaven,
   Amid the gathering gloom.

The warders pace the battled walls,
  Dark shapes against the moon ;
They challenge, and the drawbridge falls,
  The Pilgrim entereth soon.

Sleep ! Pilgrim, sleep ! for all is well !
  The dawn of Christ will break ;
When tolleth the first matin-bell,
  Pilgrim, awake, awake !

In St. Peter's Church 'tis Easter day,
  They sing the Holy Mass.
The Pilgrim Gray doth meekly pray
That here at length his sad soul may
  From fleshly bondage pass.

All in a cloud of incense sweet,
  The priests in robes of gold
Softly the Kyrië repeat,
  The solemn bell is tolled.

From his high throne the Pope steps down
  And kneels right humbly there ;
They lay aside the triple crown,
  A silence holds the air.

And in the trancéd interval,
  That seems eternity,
The Priest lifts up in sight of all
  The Sacred Host on high.

Far off and soft the organs play,
  Like heavenly psalteries :
The last chant echoes far away,
  And into silence dies.

The Pilgrim worn, with seraph eyes,
  Murmurs the holy song ;
From the watch-towers of Paradise
  Gaze down the angel-throng.

" Now lettest thou ! " his lips repeat,
 As o'er his straining view
A haze of happy memories sweet
 Gathers in tearful dew.

An odour on his senses steals,
 Like smell of fresh April :
Bird-music in his glad ear peals,
 From a green valley still.

Bright through the mist he sees them blow
 Each silver hawthorn flower,
And leaflets green that broaden slow,
 As under April shower.

And in that moment he was 'ware
 How from his golden throne
The Pope intoned the Blessing there;
 The Holy Mass is done.

Nought recks he now of earthly things;
  Only the body fain
In slumber swoons; while round him rings
  The angels' glad refrain:

    " Weary years seven
      Now are done;
     Welcome in Heaven,
      Weary one.

    " Wreath of white flower,
      Without thorn,
     They weave for thy dower,
      Pilgrim forlorn!"

ENVOI.

On earth, with little pomp, they laid
   His body poor in sod ;
One taper lit, a few prayers said,
   His soul hath rest in God.

What guerdon for the bitter tears,
   What for the weary Quest ?
The angels count those Pilgrim years,
   And God—He knoweth best !

THE BEDE OF JOHN.

An utter drought consumed the land,
  Dimmed all the golden grain
With bitter blight : quite still did stand
  The cattle on the plain,
    Weary with pain.

Then John, the lowly, gazed abroad
  At noon, with pinched face thin,
Upon his field, and sighed " O Lord !
  On two dear souls within
    Lay not my sin ! "

At eve he took the rugged way
  Across the sun-dried rill
With pain, to where he knew alway
  The great Christ hung so still
    Upon the hill.

He laid his hot brows on the stone,
  His dizzy brain spun round :
" Spare but my little field ! " his moan,
  Like waters on dry ground,
    Sank without sound.

The blight smote on the field of John,
  No cloud stirred in the sky,
His cattle faltered and fell down,
  And there each one did die,
    Beneath his eye.

Anon, for food grew scant, his wife
  Sickened, and sat alway
Staring upon the wall ; her life
  Ebbed like the fading ray
    Of a spent day.

Thereat he clomb once more the hill
  And knelt there, undismayed,
Before the great Christ white and still;
  "Only her life!" he said,
    "Her life!" he prayed.

Within the house a corpse lay stiff,
  His child wept ~~by it~~ on her knees;
So lightly passed her soul as if,
  Amid the poplar trees,
    Died out the breeze.

The Crucified was swathed in mist
  At dawn; before Him, pale
He knelt, while those pierced feet he kist:
  "My child! if all else fail,
    Let this avail!"

But that sweet maid, his dark home's light,
  Waned ever worn and wan;
Till on the midwatch of a night,
  Laid in the arms of John,
    Her breath was gone.

Tearless, the tender body dead
　　In linen white he wound,
Set on the breast a poppy red ;
　　Then laid it 'neath the ground,
　　　　And sank and swound.

With dizzy brain he clomb to where
　　Wide-armed the white Christ shone ;
With dry lips murmured this one prayer :
　　" Behold thy servant John !
　　　　Thy will be done ! "

Sunrise and sunsetting, long years,
　　Tending that way his herd,
The self-same prayer he said with tears :
　　One day he sank, nor stirred.
　　　　His prayer is heard !

At Heaven's door a sad soul waits ;
　　" Behold thy servant John ! "
It saith, and lo ! the pearly gates
　　Ope the dim dusk upon—
　　　　His will is done !

DANSE DES BACCHANTES.

Euoi ! Euoi ! Not one dark branch is stirred
Of all the dewy pines, nor one white bell
Sways of the faint narcissus ; yet they come !
For from the vale's green depths rose up a cry
Far off, which echo, huntress-like, pursued
In every chasm and twilight cave.

                    Euoi !
Hark ! how the branchéd glades ring to the shrill
Ecstatic piping of the Phrygian flute !
The wild bright cymbals clash, and swift and white
Wild arms gleam through the green, and momently
Some glad face, all o'errun with god-like joy,
Strikes on the sense like light or glint of steel.

6

A dream unveiled of white limbs leaping, foam
Of snowy breast or hand, and sumptuous wave
Of hair unbound, and dappled fawn skin, flung
O'er wine-stained shining shoulders, on they come !
The cymbals clang, thick incense fumes drift by,
They shout and sing, the unnumbered rosy lips
And full white throats, while swift, like first hot drops
O' the thunderstorm, beat quick and thick their feet
In whirlings of the fierce phrenetic dance.

Their vine-clad thyrsi wave far down the glade,
'Mid tremulous light and gloom alternately,
The wild hymn dies, faint breathe their flutes far heard,
The cymbals softlier clang ; and all are gone !

Save where one wearied Bacchant sideway flung
Lies, over-wrought with dance and ecstasy,
Her white limbs purple-stained, and eyelids soft
Slow-drooping, while her bright breast panting sighs
To the deep heavings of a dreamless sleep.

THE CHRIST OF ANDERNACH.

Ah! bitter cold and wet with mist the night,
  A dreary heaven lit by one pale star!
Strait is the street and dark, save where a light
  Before the white Christ glimmers faint and far.

"Lord! for these stones are hard, and heart of man
  Harder than stone, I lay me down to die.
No bread have I, and this poor babe's lips wan
  Turn from my wasted breasts, for they are dry.

"Lord! be thou pitiful unto my sin,
  Who art so meek of heart; life's ways are sore;
My ears are all aweary of life's din,
  Lord! I am tired! open thou Death's door!"

The flickering lamp before the Cross yet swung,
   Whereon, all naked and sore-buffeted,
The pale Christ drooped his head, and still there
     clung
   The weary woman, praying to be dead.

She slept; the first slow steps of Death drew near,
   Soft as o'er poppies strewn beneath his feet;
When one stood by her side, and in great fear
   The lost one lifted up her eyes to greet.

Scant covering had that stranger from the wind,
   The drizzling mist dropped from his long thick
     hair,
And on that lost one crouching were inclined
   Eyes wet with sorrow, but surpassing fair.

One hand he reached, 'twas wounded in the palm :
" Bread for thy child and thee ! Behold I mourn
With those that mourn ; my sorrows are the balm
   For toil-worn feet and hearts by anguish torn."

He blest and passed, and lo! the light was gone,
    That ever burned before the dead Christ there;
And gazing upward, through the moonhaze shown,
    Cold, stark, and drear, she saw the Cross was
        bare.

Whereat with one loud cry she swooned and lay
    Before the Cross; and one, who heard the cry,
Looked forth into the street, where now the day
    Made blank and pale the spaces of the sky

And lo! before the Cross a ladder set,
    And one mounts up and hangs the lamp thereby;
And stretching arms of love with night dews wet,
    Bows down in death on that new Calvary.

A SPRING REVERIE.

A LONELY spire beside the river,
  Dark on the grey sky's monotone,
Beside the stream, whose windings quiver
  With gleams that linger and are gone.

The sun glints through a misty veil
  Upon the steep road wet with rain,
That gleams like burnished silver pale,
  Embossed with many a wandering vein.

O'er all the distance vague and sweet
  Dreams the dim promise of the spring :
The spring, the spring ! my lips repeat,
  My heart exults and strives to sing.

The trees stand bleak with branches bare,
    And yet I know that spring is nigh,
By this soft circumambient air,
    Circling in mellow mystery.

No primrose stars the dun wet slopes,
    Cowslip, or bright March daffodil:
This is the hour of half-formed hopes,
    Hid in the future vast and still.

Arouse, my heart! the winter fades,
    The frost is o'er, the spring's glad song
Shall waken all these barren glades,
    And vacant meadow space ere long.

O wondrous woof of sight and sound,
    Woven around from waking hours,
Behold me by thy magic bound,
    A willing captive to thy powers!

These subtle scents and colours fine,
　　With every phase of thy great life,
O Nature, mould my soul with thine,
　　Peace with thy peace, strife with thy strife.

When those I loved, with bitter words
　　And hostile glances turned aside,
Solace came to me from thy birds,
　　And rest, close nestling to thy side.

Not ever thus, as in some shrine,
　　Dost thou with open face confer ;
As if some sacrament divine
　　Thy presence did administer.

Day wearies and the night draws nigh ;
　　Kindle thy mighty lamps, and set
Thy starry watch-fires in the sky,
　　Seals of a love that watches yet !

LOVE'S REQUIEM.

MARIE.

" THE garden-close is bright with heat,
    That wafts a cloud of odours faint
From beds of flowers ; the hot rays beat
    In dazing hues through the blazoned saint !
I can only lie in this broidered chair,
And lean my head, and gasp for air !"

RÉNÉ.

" Then lift thy white face, pale Marie,
    From its cloudy nest of tresses dark :
I close with care the jalousie,
    So that never a single garish spark
Can steal into the scented gloom
Of this tapestry-hung and silent room."

MARIE.

" This sudden shroud on the sun's hot glare
    Makes dim the scroll before mine eyes :
Blue spots and green dance in the air,
    Like a swarm of painted dragon-flies.
Then how can I read the notes aright
In this close chamber, devoid of light ? "

RÉNÉ.

" Let not that thought distress thee more ;
    For lo ! in its cavern of ivory
I kindle the silver lamp, before
    This dim old picture, pale Marie.
Now let thy song flow free and bold,
In waves and rivulets of gold."

MARIE.

" My lips are parched : they strive in vain !
    My throat is like a fountain dry
In a desert land, which yearns for rain
    That falls not from a cloudless sky,
Or as at noon the nightingale
Is athirst for dews and moonlight pale."

RÉNÉ.

"Set thy parched mouth to this cup of gold,
    Where white snow melts in the wine blood red!
Drink deep! nor let thy lips withhold,
    Until thy thirst be comforted!
Then let thy voice, pale Marie mine,
Flow full and free, like outpoured wine!"

MARIE.

"But see! I cannot, for a string
    Hath snapped and shivered in the lute.
How to thy measures might I sing,
    If one sweet silver wire be mute?
That would make discord harsh for love,
The peacock shrieking to the dove!"

RÉNÉ.

"See, I reset the broken wire!
    Now list! O languid pale Marie,
How swift and clear, like rising fire,
    The notes ascend in harmony!
Then linger not, my lady, pray,
Thy slim hand's cunning to essay!"

MARIE.

" Thou wilt not heed !   Then list, and hear
    Marred music of my heart's unrest !
  The discords jar upon thine ear ?
    My heart is broken in my breast !
  Death plays the only psaltery,
  That hath a charm for pale Marie ! "

BENEDICITE.

Cecily, Gertrude and Aloÿse
Lay in the shade of the orchard trees.
Fair are the blossoms that blow in the Spring !

Bright-haired and comely, as may be seen,
Clad all in purple and velvet green.
Fair are the blossoms that blow in the Spring !

The apple-blooms drift down, pink and white,
Through April shadow and April light.
Fair are the blossoms that blow in the Spring !

"Heigh ho! right fair is the world to see!"
Sung Gertrude loud to Cecily.
Fair are the blossoms that blow in the Spring!

Father Austin passed by the orchard wall:
Lightly the maidens to him did call.
Fair are the blossoms that blow in the Spring!

With eyes downcast on his Breviary,
Father Austin gave " Benedicite!"
Fair are the blossoms that blow in the Spring!

"O! prayers are well for a shaven head,
And shrift is the balm for a death-bed!"
Fair are the blossoms that blow in the Spring!

Then they laughed and sang to the sky above
"O heart, true heart, thou hast my love!"
Fair are the blossoms that blow in the Spring!

*   *   *   *

Father Austin passed by the orchard wall ;
But no sweet voices to him did call.
Where are the blossoms that blew last Spring ?

The withered leaves drift down and blow
On three green graves, set all a-row.
Where are the blossoms that blew last Spring ?

By tapers' shine they chant for them
In the Abbey dim a Requiem.
Where are the blossoms that blew last Spring ?

Their bodies three are laid full low ;
But where their souls be, who may know ?
Where are the blossoms that blew last Spring ?

LAC D'AMOUR.

MORN pales above thee mistily,
And far as any eye can see,
The shining water-spaces gleam
Lucid and grey, as in a dream.
The silver water-lilies float
With broad dark leaves upon the moat ;
Far out a single swan scarce stirs
The lake with that white breast of hers
And ruffled plumage, drifting by
O'er still reflections of the sky.
Midway a low-built bridge of stone
Runs o'er, and mirrored there alone
A time-beat tower stands bleak and grim
Against the grey horizon dim.

Where be the loves which gave thee name ?
All perished is the rosy flame
That lit those bygone centuries :
Nought save their ashen memories,
Unrecked of man, breathe round thy marge !

Did here, at midnight, some dark barge
Steal up unto yon lonely tower,
And music-wooed from out her bower
A maiden fair yearn down upon
The passionate face she had undone ?
Or through these rustling reeds did come,
By dawn, some youth to hear his doom
Breathed forth from rosy faltering lips ?
If so, 'tis hid in time's eclipse.

I, rather, musing, love to dream,
That deep in the uncertain gleam
Of these wan waters dwells a sprite,
And through the watches of the night

She sings of love, and doth unfurl
Moon-coloured hair with comb of pearl.
Far down beneath the shadowy mere,
Five fathom deep, in water clear,
They sleep on beds of river bloom,
The men she lured unto their doom.

Howbeit, whatever dead romaunt
Of love doth thy pale waters haunt,
Vague lake ! like thee, the calm grey years
Lie hushed of vain desire and tears,
Calm and unvexed by any wind.

What issue of the passion blind,
The wild caresses, tear-stained eyes,
And sad hearts rent by sacrifice ?

Fit image of the past, dim shore
And shadowy water, Lac d'Amour !

MUSIC OF THE SPHERES.

I LAY upon a heathery crag at noon,
   And o'er the crystal blue,
And o'er the phantom-wraith of the dead moon
   Rain-vapours drew.

O'er the rent rocks and the green vale, where swept
   In silver curves the stream,
And o'er the seven vague distant hills there crept
   A wan rain-dream.

From ruddy crag and emerald slopes of vine
   Their colours died away,
From opal arch of heaven the clear sunshine,
   Till all was gray.

7 *

Then, on a sudden, the great sun grew strong,
   And, like a sword of light,
The river flashed from out its scabbard, long
   And keen and bright.

The mountains slow unveil their purple head,
   The vineyards glitter gold,
With glory of purple heather and granite red
   The crags unfold.

Then on my beating heart, like angel's tears,
   Or drops of faery dew,
There fell the music of the crystal spheres,
   Thrilling me through

With pleasure deepening into pain, until
   Pleasure grew out of pain ;
It penetrated all the vale and hill
   With a clear rain

Of melody, more sweet than in moonlight
    Echoes a god-struck lyre,
'Mid olive woods on a Thessalian night,
    Strung with desire.

My soul was as a woof of thinnest mist
    Which the sun's burning flame
And passion burn, and the keen dews have kist,
    And sunset's shame,

And multitudinous stars and white moon-rays,
    With web of pearly dreams
Have swathed, ere yet the garish swift-foot days
    Bring back their beams.

My soul hung o'er the deeps of mystery;
    Yet how may tongue express
The varying music of the melody,
    Its loveliness?

It brought to mind dim caves in unknown seas,
   Haunted by ghostly foam,
And boundless forests of rich-blossomed trees,
   Where no men come,

But all its endless glades are wreathed in bloom
   And loud with throbbing song;
Music like this drew that proud city of doom,
   Her gateways strong,

Pale palaces and white magnificence,
   Cloud-like from Ilion's plain :
Delight so exquisite and so intense
   Is sharpest pain !

On, as a mountain runs with rifted light
   And sheets of dazzling snow
And violet ice, up to a central height
   From lakes below:

So with up-gathered strength the melody,
  Circling, swept round and round,
And culminated in an ecstasy,
  A point of sound.

Then scattered like a billow's shattered spray
  Dissolved in rainbow light,
It faltered on the winds of heaven astray,
  Shorn of its might.

Soft as the falling of a seraph's tears,
  Or drops of faery dew,
Rapt into silence, music of the spheres,
  Adieu! Adieu!

THE DEATH OF TIME.

Upon a white moon crag, that, like a wraith,
Glimmers amid th' aerial crystal waste,
Where after the red surge of ruin spreads
A silent yawning chasm of atmosphere,
Hangs ancient Time, clutching its topmost peak
With drooping pinions whiter than sea-foam.

Hollow his eyes, that through his scattered locks
Glow, like a lamp expiring in the gloom.
His half-shut lips, with writhing effort, strive
To syllable the word Eternity,
But only vent strange murmurings that fade
In that fine deluge of unmeasured air.

Slowly his tense grip loosens, and he glares
Adown the abyss of awful nothingness,
Where that sharp peak runs out like a keen sword.
His eyes are kindled in a last weird flame,
His parched lips move, as with an extreme breath
They echo forth the dread Eternity.

Then with rent pinions, like distorted cloud,
And glitter of his moonlight scythe, Time falls
Down, down into the Infinite Eterne !

A NORTHERN FANTASY.

SHE sits far off and dreams,
  Her laughter shrilly climbs
The chill stars' woven beams,
  Like silver-changing chimes,
Around her circling gleams
  The mist of bygone times.

Bright shameless marigolds
  Enwreathe her glistening hair,
Pale jewels clasp the folds
  About her shoulders fair,
Her listless right hand holds
  The courses of the air.

The monstrous snake that lies
   Around the gleaming world,
With dull unchanging eyes
   Beneath her feet is curled ;
The while her deft hand plies
   The tempest-woof unfurled.

A dead eternal light
   Broods round her pearly seat,
And in wild dances bright
   Red northern fires compete ;
Seldom in wan long flight
   White northern sea-wings beat.

Above in jewelled sleep
   The million ice-peaks loom
Through veils of mist that creep
   Over their lustrous bloom,
And in their ravines deep
   Resound her songs of doom.

Ever through airy veils,
  Her bright ice-spindle speeds,
And her sweet song not fails,
  Careless of earth's wild needs—
What, though a mother wails,
  Or many a nation bleeds ?

Some day, they say, in fire
  And glare of ruin fell
Shall perish her desire,
  With every magic spell,
Consumed on lurid pyre—
  I know not : who can tell ?

THE PALMER GREY.

A PALMER's staff was in his hand,
Grey palmer's weeds he wore,
With sandal shoon, from Holy Land,
He trod fair England's shore.
In pious zest
He smote his breast,
And said "Confiteor!"

The merry, merry hunt was out,
The hunter's horn rang free;
With horse and hound the blithesome rout
Flashed by him on the lea.
He bent his head,
And softly said
Another "Hail, Marie!"

With solemn pace he walked beside
　　The streamlet's mossy rim,
Where lovers twain sat side by side,
　　And reckoned nought of him.
　　　　With stifled moan,
　　　　He did intone
A penitential hymn.

Upon the white high-road he met
　　A merchant, with his train
Of bales of silk on palfreys set,
　　And glare of jewels vain.
　　　　He turned and sighed,
　　　　" Ah ! this world's pride
Is dust upon the plain ! "

At close of eve the holy man
　　Within a stone chapell
Laid down his burthen for a span,
　　That he his beads might tell.

Three psalms he said
For newly dead
At " De Profundis " bell.

Eftsoon the hunters wending slow
   Rode by in sorry plight ;
Nor beast nor bird they found, I trow,
   From dawn to fall of night.
      In that dim place
      They saw his face
Shine, as an angel's bright.

The lovers eke passed by the place,
   But strange and far apart,
With sullen frowns upon each face,
   And daggers in each heart.
      " Alack ! " he sighed,
      " The rose doth hide
The sharp thorn's bitter smart ! "

When that the midnight moon did rise,
　　Two wounded henchmen bore
The merchant rich, in dying guise,
　　Unto the chapell door.
　　　　With bated breath
　　　　He whispereth,
　"Yea !　Blessed are the Poor !"

At break of day three woodmen found
　　The Palmer kneeling there,
All stark in death upon the ground
　　With hands clasped as in prayer.
　　　　In greenwood glade
　　　　His corse they laid—
　His soul was otherwhere.

BABEL.

Hushed into stillness lay the midnight plain,
And dark against the purple sky
In lonely majesty
Towered that wondrous pile, the effort vain
Of a mad world to live in memory.
Rising in tier on tier, and yet again
In gallery on golden gallery,
Sombre and still the proud presumptuous mass
Awaited the loud tumult and the hand
Of countless workers yet to overpass
All bounds of time, mortality, to stand
Its head among the planets' whirl, its base
Firm-fixed to be the wonder of each land.

Around the sides ran sculptured fair
Old stories of primæval world,
The dark earth wondering at the starry line,
The glory of the orb of day, and there
Those heaven-aspiring angels earthward hurled ;
And rich and rare
The storied walls rose upward, with a stair
Enwreathed around them, like the vine
Close to the windy elm-tree curled,
And drooping in the pauses of the wind
Her sunny leaves about the glowing bunches twined.

Far as the verge of sky did reach
    The tented myriads lay,
Innumerous as on the beach
    In some deep-brooding bay,
Before the confusion and rush of the wind
    The storm breakers burst in feathery spray,
And prelude the fury that lingers behind
    The utter cloud-darkness in battle array.

Is it a star ?   A star ?

  Or meteor rushing bright ?

That shines where constellations are

  And grows in light :

Opening, opening like a rose,

Wings are beating the gloom, and close

And closer an angel silvery white,

With thunder under his feet,

With the beat

Of thunder under his wingéd feet.

He stands on the tower, his eagle eyes

Are fixed on the slumbering plain ;

He sees the farthest tent that lies

Dimly shown,

And the wilderness lone,

Beyond the uttermost mortal gaze :

  Then his hand he lays

On the crown incomplete of the tower : the rays

Of the dawn touched his wings, as in thunder he says

8 *

" The swift-footed days
Have numbered a time and half a time;
The Author sublime
Hath scattered thy glory and shattered thy praise.

" Confusion and tumult henceforth be thy name,
And the flame
Of discord sever with Babel of sound,
And the flying of camels to find
A land beyond the sun's golden bound,
And to speed on the wings of each hurrying wind,
Till after many mad wildering years
All ocean and earth be calmed, and the blind
Struggle after the vain be lost, and all tears
Wiped away in the love of the Infinite Mind,
And the flush of the morning that never dies
From the roseate depths of marvellous skies."

A flash in the night!   He is gone!
And the plain,

Where the morning is cleaving his way alone
From under a fire-fringed cloud, with a sword
Dew-dripping, and scattering diamond rain,
Far abroad
Is shaken with rushing hurrying feet,
And a clamour as loud as the cry that is blown
From the ocean-line of birds, as they beat
The wild breeze,
That roars from over the wind-driven seas ;
When they seek, like an arrow, voluptuous lands
Of low red sunsets and gold-scattered sands,
Where over the valley the mountain stands,
And the incense of flowers ascends to God,
Where the shadowy spirit of morning hath trod.

Madly they glared at each other, the blast
Of Heaven's displeasure cold-withering blew ;
And at last
The long laden line of camels swift flew,
Some east and some west ;

And the babel of sound,

All the still-blazing noon,

Roared ever around

The motionless pile, till the moon

Gazed down on that ruin of hopes, and the ground

Bestrewn with the weary unable to fly,

Over all the deep sky,

And the fire-panting stars that never can die.

LORDSMAN AND LADY.

A LORDSMAN went a-wayfaring,
To gather tithes at harvesting ;
A good man he and true of word,
Well loved withal by serf and lord
For justice strait and charity,
Albeit a bended brow had he.

This autumn eve it chanced that slow
Homeward he rode through sunset glow
Upon his sorrel palfrey, clad
In amice furred of colour sad :
Within the leathern scrip, that hung
About his neck, gold coins rung.

The silence, that the falling year
Oft hath, possessed him.   Sharp and clear
His horse's hoofs rang out upon
The white high road, till gladly won
The green sward, smooth as velvet, sank
Adown the wood by mossy bank.

Quite still and dim the forest seemed ;
Yet where he needs must pass there gleamed
Keen steel amid the bracken red,
Wherein three thieves lay ambushéd.

Musing he rode, his reins let fall
Upon his horse's mane ; the call
Of thrush and corncrake sounded faint :
Anon all rich with storied saint
He drew from vest his Psalter Book.
It was a way he ne'er forsook,
Each day upon his bended knee
To say our Lady's Psaltery.
That livelong day his business
Had hindered with unwonted stress,

So now he tethered there his steed,
Knelt down, and straight began his bede.

The robbers watch him there dismount,
And his devotions tell ; they count
Impatient, every " ave " told
Fulfilled with cruel greed of gold.
E'en as he prayed in that dim place,
A light broke o'er the earnest face,
Transfigured quite ; and lo ! there stood
Beside him in the lonely wood,
With mantle blue, a lady fair !
And as the good man told his prayer,
She laid a chaplet on his head,
And soft with each low ave said,
Set in the wreath a rose so bright
The darksome wood was filled with light :
Then when his prayers all finished are
He kissed the earth for *Venia*,
The lady parted therewithal.

Straightway the thieves upon him fall
And hale the lordsman to their lair.
Some shadowed splendour of that prayer
Yet lingered in his wondering eyes,
Haunting them with still mysteries:
Like face of one who hath beholden
In ecstasy the portals golden
Half-open, thronged with faces keen
Of angels, such seemed his, I ween.

Ruthless they drag him to their chief;
With jealous hate the cruel thief
Chafed at such innocence, his no more,
Minding him how in days of yore
He lispéd at a mother's knees
With childish lips such prayers as these.

He smote the lordsman on the cheek:
" Sir praying clerk, look up and speak !
That downcast mien thy trade avows.
What lady was it crowned thy brows

With wreaths of roses white and red ? "
Whereat the man astonishéd
Made answer : " Lady none saw I ;
For, reading in my Psaltery,
I said our Lady's lauds and nones,
Till pausing I looked upward once ;
And for my heart was cold with fear
Of these, prayed Mary Queen to hear
The cryings of her servitor."
The robber's brow was dark afore
With greed of gold : at Mary's name
He shrank, as from a touch of flame.
" Nay, for her blessed love, pardie,
Pass on thy road !   In charity
Pray for my soul unto her grace ! "
And therewithal in little space
Safe on his way the lordsman went,
Fulfilled with joy and wonderment.

Such succour may our Lady bring
To all on their life's wayfaring !

THE TOURNAMENT.

THE lists rang loud with trumpet blare
　　And shout of victory, the last thrust
　　Had laid the last knight in the dust
That eddied yet in the hot air.

'Mid all that wave of helm gone down
　　And shorn white plume he sat upright,
　　And on his pale lips came a light,
And from his brows died out the frown.

High on his lance-head flashed and swung
　　The tourney's death-won diadem;
　　The ladies smiled; he glanced at them
Leaning athwart the barriers hung

With loom of Ind enwoven rich
 In bird and flower; and there serene,
 Cheeks triumph-flushed, the tourney queen
Sat in her deep embroidered niche.

Silent a moment, thus he gazed
 On all that beauty and the loud
 Upturned white faces of the crowd,
Askance, and sight and ears were dazed.

Then crying loud : " The meed of Love
 For her the victor deems most fair,
 My Lady; I must seek her *there!* "
He pointed to the heaven above,

That blue as any gem lay spread :
 With frantic shout they mocked and jeered
 " The Dastard ! "—they who lately cheered.
He answered nought, but bowed his head.

Then forth they drove him from the list
　　With ribald shout and missile vile ;
　　Yet none the less his clear eyes smile ;
He rode from out the gate : they hissed.

ST. VALENTINE'S EVE.

THE moon shines faint, the winds are low,
  The pearly cloudlets, one by one,
Fleet o'er her face full sad and slow;
  Before moon-set my task be done.
Marjoram and balsam sweet,
  Strew them on my true love's breast;
Stone at head, and turf at feet,
  Low she lies in dreamless rest.

My love lies 'neath the black yew-tree
  (Softly tread or she will wake!)

Soft the shadows pass and flee ;
 Softly or the charm will break.
Marjoram and balsam sweet
 Strew them on my true love's breast ;
Stone at head, and turf at feet,
 Low she lies in dreamless rest.

'Neath the sod my love sleeps sound,
 All alone by the dark church-tower ;
Softly tread and strew around
 Marjoram and gilly-flower.
Marjoram and balsam sweet,
 Strew them on my true love's breast ;
Stone at head, and turf at feet,
 Low she lies in dreamless rest.

Wildly now my heart doth beat ;
 Hark ! the church bell deep doth toll ;
Rest is all that I entreat,
 Rest like thine, thou sainted soul !

Marjoram and balsam sweet,
　Strew them on my true love's breast;
Stone at head, and turf at feet,
　Low she lies in dreamless rest.

Here I lay me down beside:
　This green turf is softest bed;
Sleep will come at thy dear side,
　Churchyard mound beneath my head.
Marjoram and balsam sweet,
　Strew them on my true love's breast;
Stone at head, and turf at feet,
　Low she lies in dreamless rest.

The morrow is St. Valentine;
　At the dawn our lips shall greet,
When the first pale ray doth shine
　On the daisies at thy feet!
Marjoram and balsam sweet,
　Strew them on my true love's breast;

9

Stone at head, and turf at feet,
  Low she lies in dreamless rest.

Sweet thy slumber 'neath the sod,
  Sweetheart now no more adieu;
We shall wake and be with God,
  Close together, I and you!
Marjoram and balsam sweet,
  Strew them on my true love's breast;
Stone at head, and turf at feet,
  Low she lies in dreamless rest.

LYRICS,

&c.

EPHEMERA.

A DELICATE ripple of sunlight,
  Quenched in an April gloom ;
Faint-fluttering petals drifted
  From the latest pale rose-bloom ;
A phantom glimmer of twilight,
  Revealing a darkened room.

The jewelled mist of a rainbow,
  When the sun and the rain-storm meet ;
Vibrations of exquisite music,
  As the lute-strings cease to beat ;
Things lovely and evanescent—
  Oh ! wherefore are these things sweet ?

PROEMION.

WHERE the priestess stands and showers
  Keen salt on the crackling fire,
White and red-hearted flowers
  Are strewn for the god's desire.

A few faint rose leaves fluttered
  On the marble altar base ;
A few swift fancies uttered
  In the heart's most holy place.

As the dewy petals drifted
  Are fraught with an odour of prayer,
These songs with the solemn are gifted,
  And laid on Life's altar-stair,
          To wither there !

THE RING.

I HAD a ring that unto me seemed fair,
  So many rainbow lights dwelt in the gem ;
So strangely wrought the setting rich and rare :
  Yet few e'er praised it, when I showed it them.

And years I treasured it for my delight,
  And oft-times rising in the early morn
Would joy to see its inner fires grow bright,
  And redden through faint opal like the dawn.

Or at noontide behold it flash and burn
  And tremble, like a flame blown divers ways ;
But most at night within my palm to turn
  The stone that in the moon enwove wan rays.

Now seemed it like a faded sapphire, now
   Pale emerald, topaz, or the beryl stone :
Till seeing this, my friend did straight avow
   I did great wrong to hoard my joy alone.

" Nay, let it sparkle in men's eyes, and so
   Shall it win wonder and its beauty's meed."
This saying troubled me, I answered low :
   " Why let all careless eyes their glances feed

" Upon my treasure, fair indeed to me ;
   But to all those, who have not loving eyes
To see the glamours that mine own eyes see,
   My well-loved gem will seem a worthless prize !

Such words in haste I spake : " Give me the ring ! "
   With voice reproachful murmured that dear
      friend ;
" I prize it, though it be no precious thing."
   And so I gave it him to make an end.

HIRONDELLES.

Love came with the wild sweet swallow,
On a wild March day,
To abide for the summers that follow,
Alway.

While the green still hours of summer
Glided softly away,
He abode, that blithe new-comer,
Alway.

When the last pale roses were dying,
And skies grew grey,
Love spread his wings, and was flying
Away.

The spring will come back, and the swallow
    Return some day :
But alack for a love found hollow
    Alway !

VALENTINE.

My Valentine !
    All of pale violets,
Fit for Love's shrine,
My valentine.
Love in a line
    Is the law of these Triolets;
My valentine,
    All of pale violets !

THE QUESTION.

You glanced at me last night,
  And heaven looked through:
This dark world would be bright,
  If it were true.

The pressure of your hand
  To bid adieu
Would unlock fairy-land,
  If it were true.

The heartsease at your breast,
  Purple and blue,
Looked up from that sweet rest,
  As if they knew.

Bright sudden splendid gleams
  Build earth anew :
If these be but fair dreams,
  Oh tell me true !

ABSENCE.

Could you but guess the longing vain,
   The aching weary restlessness,
Until I see your face again,
     Could you but guess!

Parted from you, all empty seems;
   The moment that I bid adieu,
Fade from the earth its fairy gleams,
     Parted from you!

What time we meet, the earth grows bright;
   Round me the air is faint and sweet,
And radiant with a mystic light,
     What time we meet!

LOVE'S CROWN.

O! BRING for my love a coronet,
   Aflame from Dawn's pale throne,
With jewelled fires in a golden fret,
     Beryl-stone :

And casting back Love's own rose light
   From my Lady's sovereign face,
With inner fires that kindle bright,
     Chrysophrase :

And soft as a spray of lilac bloom,
   Seen through an April mist,
Or a star, dissolved in night's blue gloom,
     Amethyst :

Go, then, sweet angel ministers,
Smite each your silver lyre,
And crown that royal brow of hers,
Heart's desire!

NOCTURNE.

The night is soft, a tender haze
    Bedims the stars,
    Through cloudy bars
The moon doth seaward gaze,
And all the wandering ocean-ways
Are touched and kindled by her beams,
The while this shadowy shore I pace in dreams.

The moon-white spray upon the rocks is thrown,
   And quivering like a lyre
Each separate wave this way and that is blown
   In tremulous shafts of fire.

A shade steals o'er the heaven,
　The lonely vast
Looms dim, until the cloudy woof is riven,
　And light is cast
Far over rock-bound shore and ocean pale ;
Then slow once more the brilliance soft doth fail.

The steep town sleeps in night,
　But blurs of golden flame
Burn here and there in windows bright.
　O ! joy I scarce dare name,
Yonder her chamber's rosy light,
Love's beacon-star beams on my gladdened sight.

O ! for a fairy lute,
　Strung from the silver spray,
Whereof no string is mute :
　Love's roundelay
Might then sigh on amid this hueless air,
Night's secret passion throbbing in my prayer.

TOO LATE.

O ! sweet pale face,
  I saw you first,
As in some dim place
  A sudden burst
Of orange flower at twilight seen
Amid the deep leaves' sombre green.

Pure, virginal,
  Close-folded yet,
The Spring's sweet call
  And warm tears wet
Had not yet wooed into a star
Of odorous white the bud's close bar.

10 *

" I will return,
  Some other morn,
When rich suns burn
  And fruits are born,
Warm, golden-red, and ripe at last
Ere summer hours be overpast."

I came elate
  To pluck my prize ;
I came too late,
  For other eyes
Had marked my gold fruit hanging there,
And nought was left on branches bare !

PENUMBRA.

One more kiss, love !   Even Death
  Cannot rob our lips of this !
One more touch of that dear breath,
  One more kiss !

O ! dear eyes I know so well,
  Shadowed by that cloud of hair,
With love's self, as in a well,
  Mirrored there.

Yes ! you whisper we shall meet
  Far beyond in some dim land,
Recognize and gently greet,
  Hand in hand.

So you say, but still a fear
   Haunts me with foreboding strange ;
Will the face I worshipped here
   Suffer change ?

SPRING.

THE snow hangs thick upon the fir
And on the grass ; no wind doth stir
The smooth gray waters of the stream,
That through the cedar-branches gleam.
Beneath the cedar one gem lies
Of emerald sod ; the wintry skies
Are white and clear and crystalline ;
No azure spaces laugh and shine.

And yet I know, beneath the snow
   Snowdrop and golden aconite
Full faintly blow, or brightly glow,
   Like burnished gold or silver bright !

And ivy buds are breaking forth,
  And yellow jessamine's pale stars
Peer out, albeit the bitter north
  Breathes blight, and swift their beauty mars.

And yesterday, his first wild lay
  I heard the fluting throstle sing:
Through barren wood and coppice stray
  The first faint footfalls of the Spring.

Soon the season of snows will be over,
The mantle of winter will slowly discover,
And primrose and snowdrop and daffodil
Will star the valley and crown the hill!

Half-fulfilled and incomplete,
I love this season of promise sweet;
The vague uncertain lights that linger
  One shadowy moment and are gone;
It stirs the heart of bird and singer,
  And lends enchantment to their tone.

Whatever lips thy glories sing,
   Summer, or Autumn golden-deep,
My hymns be thine ethereal Spring,
   Light after night, life after sleep!

A SPRING ODE.

THERE is a brightness in the new-born year,
A light and beauty in the budding leaf,
 Which softens grief,
And with a hallowed strength restrains the tear.
 I know not what it is,
 This bounding heart of joy,
Or whence flows down this plenteousness of bliss,
  Without alloy.
 Is it that Winter's ice
 And whirling snows and mist
 And bleak cold now desist?
Or is it that the summer-guerdoning spice,
 Which blows around the cheek,
 Of joys to come doth speak?
Or is it of our coursing blood some natural freak?

Over the blackthorn brake
Blossom the faery clusters white,
And sunny-bright
The daffodil flutters a golden flake,
In winds of gusty March.
Among the withered leaflets dead,
Where the fresh sap runs through the oak and larch,
Lo the faint-scented primrose lifts its head !

The hedge-rows burgeon green,
And fresher are the meads.
The lambkins frisk and leap in the gay sheen,
And the mother watchful feeds.
Under a blue sky flecked
With racing clouds, ripple the loosened streams.
The cuckoo's far-off note
Sounds as in happy dreams.
Joyous the lark doth soar and float,
And his sky-piercing song is heard the while,
As in the meadows decked
The shepherd woos his love beside the mossy stile.

All this, all this, I love !
I loved, when still
A child I sought the woodland grove,
And did my eager hands with flowers fill.

Nor was my heart content ;
For each beyond seemed a delight more fair,
Till on the ground wearied I sank and spent. ,

Here thick the blue-bells in the grass
Lie like a drifted azure cloud.
To all the winds that o'er the marish pass,
The iris slow unfurls his purple banner proud.

Why wail for what is gone ?
Still blows for me the fruitful air,
Still where the cawing rookery clusters tall,
I love to see the April violet.

It stirs no vain regret,
Though one by one the vanished summers fall.

Life is but just begun ;
And all my thoughts are like yon changeful heaven,
Now bright with sun,
Now curtained o'er by gloom and tempest-driven.

I know not why my bliss !
Is it that life for me
Hath bloomed from out the dark abyss
Of all that is to be ?
Or that when young my thought,
I joy to dream in hope of fuller strength,
Of all life's powers to their highest brought
And great at length ?

For yet the world is young,
Still in her mighty veins bounds fiery blood.
Glories there are unsung,
And many a noblest theme for bard in noblest mood.
Ocean's loud-sounding shore,
And roaring tract of darkest flood
Can now divide no more !
Beneath the wave the magic message flies !
Behold the risen crowds, the god-like poor,
As o'er each waking land oppression slowly dies !

Come, stand with me above the level marsh,
And gaze from here upon the windy sea,

And listen to the billow's music harsh,
Where on the yellow strand the foam flies free.
Lo ! as yon opal distance dimly deep,
Where sky and ocean meet,
As fully vast
Stretches the boundless years' unfettered sweep,
Of which but the first waves are at our feet :
Like yonder hill-girt marsh lies the forgotten past.

AUTUMN LEAVES.

AUTUMN leaves are whirling fast,
   Summer days are over and done:
But oh for the golden hours fled past
   And the years that are flown and gone.

The flowers hang heavy with petals wet,
   Heartsease and faint pale rose:
Sad heart lie still, and strive to forget
   The hours that the years foreclose.

Faded flowers of the heart's lost peace,
   Golden occasions fled,
Blighted promise of bright increase,
   And hope down-trodden and dead.

The sad eyes fill and brim with tears
  For the promise of bygone Spring,
Made void by the flight of the eddying years,
  In the wind of Time's wild wing.

REST.

WILD passionate heart dost thou tire
  In the prison-house of my breast?
World-wearied, what is thy desire,
  Rest? Aye Rest!

Aching eyes, aweary of day
  And glamour of colour deep,
What boon shall thy pain allay,
  Sleep? Aye Sleep!

Tired body and soul of mine,
  That groaneth and travaileth,
What well-loved guerdon is thine,
  Death? Aye Death!

THE TARANTELLE.

THE Tarantelle ! This white road's heat
Glisters like glass ; her swift brown feet
   Glance in and out, the slim hands sway
   Unto the pipe's shrill roundelay,
While quick and loud the dull drums beat.

Swift and more swift her steps compete,
Her dark eyes glitter vague and sweet
   Through her dark hair. Away, Away !
      The Tarantelle !

Her golden anklets clash ; replete
With glow and clangour, down the street
   She whirls. Ah ! dare not to essay
   To follow where those wild feet stray !
Marvel, but shun with eyes discreet
      The Tarantelle !

THE PRODIGAL.

Is this the quest?   Yes, all around deposes
  That I have seen it in a hundred dreams,
The trellised alleys and the wildering roses,
  The cedar gloom where the white statue gleams.

The same old lichened walls and ivied gables,
  Grey timeworn dial with mosses green o'ergrown,
The flower-vases, wrought with antique fables,
  The mouldering buttress and half-open door.

Through which half-seen, gliding in graceful measure
  Amid green glooms and sunny interspace,
The light-foot stags and does, with airy measure
  Flit by, all heedless of a stranger face.

11 *

All silent, from the white doves on the tower
  To the huge mastiff on the sunbeat stair ;
The bee hangs idle in the dreaming flower,
  The peacock spreads his jewels to the air.

How stir in such a charmed and calm seclusion ?
  Nay, rather in the golden atmosphere
Gaze at those peonies in rich confusion,
  Globing their crimson blossoms bright and clear.

A fairy palace !   Sure some princess slumbers,
  Where odorous silks her tender limbs enfurl,
The while slow hours her heaving bosom numbers,
  Dark-tressed and dreaming on a bed of pearl.

And I, the Fairy Prince !   Ah no, the vision
  Melts as I gaze across the fountain's side,
And laugh aloud in sad and cold derision,
  A wrinkled Prince, who seeks a phantom Bride !

PEACE.

In the cool green deep
  The seaweed swings:
Low songs of sleep
  The curled sea sings,
And west winds harp on sea-foam strings.

In the meadows green
  And moist, the kine
Lie there serene,
  While slow decline
The Spring's pale hours we deemed divine.

In the crystal air
   The blithe birds poise,
Wide-winged; from there
   Earth's plaintive noise
Their sacred calm noway alloys.

All rest in peace ;
   Only for man
No calm surcease
   Of labour's ban,
But endless toil consumes life's span.

Mother of life,
   Breathe on my face !
Amid this strife
   Grant me thy grace,
Vision of Peace in thine high place !

A SIREN.

Siren you seem, as you sit on the sand,
  Half mystery and half glee,
Touching the chords with a magical hand
  To the music of the sea :
I feel, as I listen here where I stand,
  That a spell steals over me
From the notes that dreamily pause and flow :
" *Tazah be tazah, na be na o !* "

The grey eyes are gazing far away,
  Under her hat's broad brim,
Her dress is blue, with a kerchief gay
  ˉ Twisted in wilful whim,

O'er the dark guitar long ribands stray
　　Of a hue that is rich and dim,
While the sweet lips murmur dreamy and low,
" *Tazah be tazah, na be na o !* "

The shore is limitless, wild and bare,
　　Edged with hillocks of sand,
And the waves that ceaselessly murmur there
　　Come stealing up to the strand,
To mingle their melody with the air
　　That flows from her skilful hand,
Soft as a lullaby, dreamy and low,
" *Tazah be tazah, na be na o !* "

The sound of that weird barbaric strain
　　Brings visions strange to my mind,
A golden-red sunset and pallid plain,
　　A mother dusky and kind,
Hushing her babe, while ever again
　　That lullaby floats on the wind,
Falling and soaring and eddying low,
" *Tazah be tazah, na be na o !* "

Siren ! you draw us all from our game,
   And the ringing laughter has died,
As one by one to the circle came,
   And sank on the sand beside,
Where rippling mystical sad, the same
   Soft lullaby still replied
To the beat of the bright sea echoing low,
" *Tazah be tazah, na be na o !* "

SLEEP.

The winds have hushed the sun to rest,
   The lilies dream in twilight skies,
And those soft eyelids slowly prest
   Droop o'er thy languid eyes.

All beauty falls asleep with thee,
   Save yon unwearied lights above :
But brighter than those stars shall be
   The morrow and my love !

LIFE'S BANQUET.

WITH mournful eyes and laughter,
  In mockery of our pain,
We drain the cup, and after
  Chant low the sad refrain :
" *For all the swift hours flying*
  Chant low, chant slow and sweet ! "

We wreathe pale brows with roses,
  And greet the gleaming wine,
While time's cold shade forecloses
  The hours we deemed divine :
" *For all the swift hours dying*
  Sing low, sing slow and sweet ! "

The purple wine falls wasted
   On the marble floor serene,
And life's rich fruit half-tasted
   Is sharp with juices keen.
" *For all the swift hours flying*
   Chant low, chant slow and sweet!"

With mingled pain and pleasure
   The soft lutes throb and fail;
Their sweetest saddest measure
   To soothe can nought avail:
" *For all the swift hours dying*
   Sing low, sing slow and sweet!"

Till one veiled minstrel singeth
   Unbidden at the feast:
To one and all he bringeth
   Sleep and a dreamless rest:
" *For all the swift hours flying*
   Chant low, chant slow and sweet!"

TORCHLIGHT.

FLING roses !   Let the brazen horn
Breathe stormy joy !   Our God rides, borne
High o'er the press, that shakes like corn.
    Euoi, Bacche, Euoi, Euoi !

Young Bacchus, leaning, crowned with vine ;
Low laughter on his lips divine,
He spills the red Falernian wine.
    Euoi, Bacche, Euoi, Euoi !

The heavy incense curls and sways,
And gold glows red and jewels blaze !
Lift up, lift up the hymn of praise !
    Euoi, Bacche, Euoi, Euoi !

The clashing cymbal, pipe, and lute
Ring to the beat of many a foot.
Hark! not a single lip is mute!
    Euoi, Bacche, Euoi, Euoi!

Love! lean on me, the while your tresses
Stream o'er mine eyes in blind caresses,
And all about the mad throng presses.
    Euoi, Bacche, Euoi, Euoi!

Look up! The statue laughs, the stone
Lives in the light of torches blown
To ruddy splendour, fiercer grown!
    Euoi, Bacche, Euoi, Euoi!

The multitude foams like a sea
Of tumult golden, lean on me!
Now, for the last time, loud and free!
    Euoi, Bacche, Euoi, Euoi!

RIVER PICTURES.

O'ER the wan river-reaches smooth and deep,
In tangled wilderness the lilies sleep,
With broad curved leaves and myriad blossoms
    blown,
Dreaming in silvery mist at dawn alone.

An odorous summer evening, dark until
The rising moon o'er yonder rounded hill
Shines, like a silver lamp, that in dim halls,
Where all night long the fountain-cadence falls,
Is lifted to an ivory lattice, slow
Through eastern silks, to love that sighs below.

Tall poplar spires, dark on an evening sky,
And dark in the clear waters, that steal by,
To fall in veils of pallid foam, beneath
The ruined mill, that starry marshflowers wreath.

A watery waste, at morn, with vivid isles
Of meadow, a swollen river, sunken piles :
Far off, grey spires and wintry lights of dawn.

Waters that babble past a summer lawn,
Whose sun-flecked ripples murmur undersong ;
A boat with merry laughter thrust along
Into the water-vistas, arched with trees.

Hours, happy hours in happy haunts like these !

THE RIVER OF LOVE.

Like a river is glad Love,
   When the summer suns are burning,
And the singing waters rove,
   Where the limpid eddies turning
Glass the azure skies above :
With a murmur of delight,
Through the starry summer night,
And an under-echo born of delighted ecstasy,
Adreaming of the keen embraces of the purple sea.

Like a river is sad Love,
   When the winter winds are moaning,

And the skies stretch pale above :
  Where the thunder-floods are groaning
At the bars they cannot move :
With a roaring of despair
Through the lurid evening air,
And a tremulous clamour born of bitter agony,
For the unresponsive haven of the far-divided sea.

THE RIVER OF SONG.

THE streamlet sparkles from the side
   Of the purple mountains ;
Thus from broodings solemn glide
   Fancy's sudden fountains.

As are gleaned its thousand rills
   In silver sheaves together,
Till the river softly fills
   Its breast with lucid weather :

Verse, the gleaner, binds in one
   Bright reflective river,
Thoughts that glitter and are gone,
   Absorbed in song for ever.

SCIROCCO.

THE skies are grey and blank, the bare
  White walls and barren hillocks dream;
Far on the endless ramparts stare,
  Like breath-dimmed steel the harbours gleam.

In the blank sky a pale sun fades
  Above the long hills' far dun rim,
Shorn of his light, into the shades
  He sinks, without one gold ray dim.

A dull bell tinkles: on the slope
  The goats browse on the herbage pale,
Where o'er the rampart strays the flock,
  And into dusk their white shapes fail.

A land of placid barren rest,
  Forgetfulness and pallid peace ;
Nought left to strive for, sad, unblest,
  Without remorse in hope's surcease.

Malta, 1889.

THE NIGHTINGALE.

NIGHT shades the summer vale, and all
  The flowers sleep on yonder hill :
  Only the hollow-whispering rill
Breaks silence with its silver fall.

Peace sleeps upon the midnight air
  And hushes every stormy thought,
    While in the arms of silence caught
  Sinks every sigh and murmur there.

Her hymn to the clear stars of eve
  Sobs forth the plaintive nightingale,
  And all the thicket and the vale
Re-echo to the notes and grieve.

She warbles forth her mournful cry,
   Welled from the heart in constant flow,
   As from unceasing founts of woe,
Sprung from regret for days gone by.

Sad voice ! be still, for thoughts of years,
   Deep in the past, disturb my peace ;
   I would thy sad sweet song might cease
To fill these watching eyes with tears.

Too sad to be a voice of good ;
   Too sweet for any voice of ill,
   Mourning beside the weeping rill,
And shaded by the solemn wood.

PARTING.

For the last time ?   Even so, my dear,
　Adieu, adieu !
O, white set face without one tear,
　Adieu, adieu !

Here through the waning woods made bare
　The moon shines cold,
Sole-hung far up the fine chill air
　That girds the wold.

Your hands are cold, but mine are ice,
　And in my breast
The heart's flame burns, but cannot rise,
　Clenched and comprest.

Adieu, adieu ! this moment seems
  Time's needle point,
An agony of formless dreams
  And pain conjoint.

Your hands in mine, love !   Is it so
  True love must die,
With no heart's knell, no tears that flow
  For days gone by ?

Nay, if it be the last time, love,
  Behold this breast
Open, as those broad heavens above,
  Love's last long rest !

RONDEAU.

A BRAMBLE spray!   Now dry and sere.
I plucked it on a morning clear,
  From that bare hedge-row, where it swung,
  While your sweet graces softly rung,
For that late relique of the year,
        A bramble spray.

That night I saw its purple peer
Into your white breast's secrets, dear,
  Where hid in fluttering lace it clung,
        A bramble spray.

And as I saw you disappear
Through the dark door, in joy and fear
  One leaf I craved with faltering tongue,
  One spray with one swift smile you flung,
Now consecrated by this tear,
        A bramble spray.

MORS.

Death! Death! Death!
Cold immutable king,
Who dost thy shadow fling
  O'er all that hath a living breath!
Hollow, hollow are thine eyes!
Hollow as the world we prize,
        Death!
All this life is but a flower,
In an hour,
Fading or dead!
O monarch weird and dread!
Let us wreathe our brows with flowers,
  Laugh and sing,
Chain with music the swift hours!
        Vain thing! Vain thing!

Laugh and carol as we may,
Stands at hand the fixéd day.
Veil the face and sadly lay
The cold earth in the cold clay.

Hollow, hollow, hollow !
What is it doth follow ?
Blindest darkness without end.
Kiss thy lover, clasp thy friend,
Dip the trailing lily in wine,
Let the sparkling goblet shine !
All is vain !
Cark and pain !
Wreathe the locks with bitter bane,
Bane and rue,
For that Death must come is true !
Too true !   Too true.

JANUA VITAE.

No ! there is a music higher
  In the melody of the spheres,
  And my spirit soars and hears
    Harp-strings thrilling,
    Heaven filling,
As in glowing leaping fire
  Rosy dawn divine appears.

Higher, higher, life there is,
Where the spirit, wrapt in bliss,
Knows unutterable things,
And for ever, ever sings
Beside a crystal sea,
Whilst the swelling harmony
Surges around the golden throne.

This life is not all alone !
But that man, who dares to climb
Past the bitter waste of time,
To the lonely Pisgah height,
Sees below, in golden light,
Jordan-circled and fair to view,
The Land of Rest ;
And upon his breast
Death sinks, like an evening dew,
On the hill's highest crest ;
And God in the lone
Inaccessible stone
Will bury him deep ;
And his sleep
Will be watched o'er by angels unspeakably blest.

DEPRESSION.

Weary my heart! a hollow space of Heaven,
  Where no soft cloud-wreaths steer,
Or wind stirs, like a silent sea undriven,
  An ocean drear.

A stillness holds it, as of ilex leaves
  Hushed into boding rest;
Ere yet the red sword of the tempest cleaves
  The thunder's breast.

Weary my heart! as his who with worn eyes,
  Amid the desert glare,
Sinks under vengeful glare of changeless skies
  And sees the air

Surcharged with waving plumes of carrion birds,
  Though near at hand a well,
A ripple of water through the palms be heard :
  For him death's knell.

The merciless thoughts close in like wings of doom,
  No ray amid the night ;
Then darkness parts and through the black soul-gloom
  Streams in God's light.

LES PATINEURS.

Lo ! mid the grey-blue of yon waning sky
  The moon hangs, like a silver sickle, pale
Above the ensanguined dusk, while far and nigh
  The ice-bound streams and water-floods prevail :
  The leafless trees stand with black branches frail
There where the skaters speed like phantoms by,
And in December dreams the dim spires lie
  Above the city, where day's murmurs fail.

Over the bridge the wayfarers press on
  Swift through the frost to many a fireside bright,
Wrapt from the wind ; me only, here alone,
  This dreary eve suits better than warm light,
And my heart, cold as this insensate stone,
  Greets with dull throb the chill December night.

II.

White snow, bright skies and tract of wind-swept ice,
    Keen lucid air that thrills the brain like wine,
    And whirl of flashing feet that swift entwine
This way and that in many a strange device :
Laughter and life encircling, that suffice
    To stay the conscious soul's deep-seated range,
    And hold it void of thought's close interchange,
Gripped by the strenuous instant in a vice.

The needle-point of pleasure, without link
    Past or to come, the moment infinite !
Even as a javelin poises on the brink,
    Self-balanced up the far sun-smitten height,
One instant, ere it waver and then shrink
    Down, to be buried deep in earth's dark night.

FLOODTIDE.

GREY hueless skies and long slip islanded
  Of barren trees and manifold dome and spire,
  With one pale streak of warmest sunset-fire,
Mirrored upon the polished floods outspread.
The deep tides struggle in the river's bed,
  Surging with fierce remonstrance ever higher,
  As though their waves Lethean would aspire
To whelm yon phantom city and all her dead.

Thou desert waste of waters weltering,
  And vacant space of blank unshaded cloud,
Triumphant now—soon shall recurring Spring
  Invade these meadows with wind-trumpets loud,
And barren branch and blade break forth and sing,
  With glory of flower and April heaven avowed.

LOVE AND FANCY.

Love is the Monarch of the heart's domain,
   And from his throne, engirt by passion's slaves,
   His awful ministering sceptre waves,
Compelling all beneath his absolute reign.
Yet is there an usurper, Fancy vain,
   Armed all as Love with quiver and bright bow,
   Who leads in bondage vacant hearts that know
No higher Lord to follow in his train.

Yet is the throne of True Love set on high,
   And perdurable, his divine rose-crown
Blooms with bright blossoms that can never die:
   But False Love passeth, at the world's cold frown
His roses fade, and with a hollow sigh,
   Prone from his shattered height the God falls down.

LOVE'S VICTIM.

O Love, thou cruel tyrant of my soul,
 Flame-winged and holding keen darts in thy hand,
 Behold me bound within thine iron band,
And groaning under thy supreme control!
Yea! for I pay thee all thine uttermost toll
 Of tears and sleepless nights and bosom-sighs :
 Behold the shadowy circles of mine eyes
And hollowed cheeks that yearn to some far goal!

Have pity, Love, and ease me of my pain ;
 Bring me unto the harbour of thy rest ;
Soothe with the dulcet tones of thy refrain
 The bitter anguish of my labouring breast.
Or let me on thine altar, Love, be slain,
 With bitter perfumes and rose-garlands drest !

DEVOTIONAL.

O SALUTARIS HOSTIA.

I HAD a vision as the night drew nigh
  O'er the soft-rounded hills and hollow stream;
An arm of twilight lay along the sky,
  The trees stood dark against the yellow gleam,
And by the deep weir-pool the abbey lay
With shattered oriels, where pale nuns were wont to
    pray.

Anon there fled a wailing on the wind,
  And echoes faint phantasmal 'mid the leaves
Trembled, and in its depths the water blind
  Murmured, as when a soul in sorrow grieves,
And my limbs shook, and in the heart's chill lake
The heart's blood shuddered as when nightly terrors
    wake.

A sound of mystic singing, and a light,
   Lucid and deepening to a rosy red,
That moved along the arches richly dight,
   Athwart the grass that rustled o'er the dead,
And through the riven tracery there I saw
A marvel living wight might see in breathless awe.

For in a lifted monstrance bright as flame
   The Sacred Host gleamed white, like driven snow,
Borne by a cloud of angel wings that came,
   Bathed in a mystery of roseate glow :
And their keen faces, adoration-thrilled,
Gave vent to piercing song that those waste ruins
     filled.

With clear ecstatic notes, like heavenly dew
   Scattered around, sounded a silver bell,
And all the seraphs' pinions as they flew
   Flushed into fire as from a sunset-well,
And moving onward sank in purple dyes,
Or glittered, spangled with a million jewelled eyes.

One moment, as I lay with awe entranced,
   The vision hung above the glassy deep
And in the lucent pool its colours glanced,
   Enwoven like the splendours rich of sleep.
The anthem pealed in one expressive tone,
The bright wings flashed, and flashing died: I lay
   alone.

MARIA DESOLATA.

Three crosses set upon an Eastern hill,
  A blood-red stripe of sunset waning low,
And that white wounded body stretched so still
  Athwart thy knees, while yet the blood-drops flow.

Is this the end, O mother desolate?
  Thou, whose wide eyes gaze forth into the night,
As striving still to comprehend thy fate,
  Too strangely sad to credit thine own sight.

This for those touches of the baby hands,
  And glances when His soul spake unto thine,
These balméd grave-cloths for the swaddling bands,
  And death for sleep to seal those eyes divine!

Yea! lift the bright hair, clotted thick with gore,
   And lave the marble brow in death more dear,
While angel millions tremble and adore
   To see that kiss commingled with a tear.

Thine ears are throbbing yet with those loud cries,
   Pulsating with the blows on wood and nail:
Now all is silent under the dark skies,
   Save for yon crouching Magdalen's low wail.

Yea! close His eyes staring so blindly up
   To the unpitying skies, and cleanse the mouth
That drank so deep from out the bitter cup,
   And parched for thirst in agony of drouth.

Arouse thee, mother, from thy sorrow's trance!
   Fold after fold, like cloud or moonlit foam,
Round wounded feet and side pierced by the lance,
   They swathe thine own slain Lamb for His last
     home.

And now, O Mother, for the task is done,
   Press one last kiss upon His icy lips,
Veil o'er the sacred Face of Christ thy son,
   And shroud all Nature in one dark eclipse !

VERBUM DEI.

Sweet are the first pale flowers that begin the
golden year,
And sweet the dewy dawning with its veils of twilight
clear;
But sweeter than all blossoms or the light from out
the night
Was the first low word of Jesus, filling Mary with
delight.

When the wonder of the angels and the Star of earth's
desire
Gave the first low premonition of His hidden sacred
fire,

When lying in the radiance of our Lady's loving eyes,
Her Babe first whispers "Mother," and the mother
    first replies.

She had known of dim communion and strange
    motions in her heart,
And unfathomable knowledge where the wells of being
    start ;
But sweeter far than knowledge, or the sound of
    Gabriel's " Hail ! "
Was the cry of her Creator, was her helpless infant's
    wail.

First word and best and sweetest of the great Incar-
    nate Word,
That within her heart immaculate the mighty mother
    heard,
And laid as in a silver shrine midmost the holiest
    place,
The price of our redemption and the crown of all her
    grace.

RHYME OF THE HALIWORK FOLK.

Haliwork folk, seven in all,
Hardy for burthen, strong and tall;
Seven brethren we of noble race,
Kith and kin in limb and face :
Seven long years our feet have trod
Valley and hill with the ark of God.

Hallowéd burthen for wayfaring
Far and wide our shoulders bring,
Hallowéd body of Cuthbert saint,
Swathed in vesture of purple faint,
Wrought with gold flowers cunningly,
Marvel great for eyes to see.

14

Hallowéd body, whole and sound,
As though our Father slept or swound;
Nor cark nor sign of corruption
That blessèd flesh may light upon;
Enwrapt in linen fine and sweet
From crown of head to sole of feet.

Hallowéd body, ark of God,
Hallowéd blossom of Aaron's rod,
Hallowéd temple, gate divine,
Saint of God and purity's shrine,
Pillar of cloud by noonday light,
Beacon of fire in dark of night!

Vouchsafe to us, thou blissful saint,
Who have borne thee far and faint,
When done life's travail and journeying,
To realms on high our souls to bring,
With endless bliss and benison,
Through bitter passion of God's dear Son!

Amen my heart doth say to it,
Whose pen this holy rhyme hath writ:
Oh! Mary, mother of fair mercy;
St. Cuthbert, likewise, pray for me!
And "gloria" be in the uttermost
To Father, Son, and Holy Ghost!

LONDON :

PRINTED BY W. H. ALLEN AND CO., 13 WATERLOO PLACE,

PALL MALL.   S.W.

www.ingramcontent.com/pod-product-compliance
Lightning Source LLC
Chambersburg PA
CBHW030324270326
41926CB00010B/1494